PROVIDING
FOR INDIVIDUAL
DIFFERENCES
IN STUDENT LEARNING
A Mastery Learning Approach

PROVIDING
FOR INDIVIDUAL
DIFFERENCES
IN STUDENT LEARNING

A Mastery Learning Approach

By

JACKSON F. LEE, JR., Ed.D.

Associate Professor
Department of Education
Francis Marion College
Florence, South Carolina

K. WAYNE PRUITT, Ed.D.

Associate Professor
Department of Education
Francis Marion College
Florence, South Carolina

CHARLES C THOMAS • PUBLISHER
Springfield • Illinois • U.S.A.

Published and Distributed Throughout the World by

CHARLES C THOMAS • PUBLISHER

2600 South First Street

Springfield, Illinois 62717

© *1984 by* CHARLES C THOMAS • PUBLISHER

ISBN 0-398-05028-7

Library of Congress Catalog Card Number: 84-2516

With THOMAS BOOKS *careful attention is given to all details of manufacturing and
design. It is the Publisher's desire to present books that are satisfactory as to their physical
qualities and artistic possibilities and appropriate for their particular use.* THOMAS
BOOKS *will be true to those laws of quality that assure a good name and good will.*

Printed in the United States of America
Q-R-3

Library of Congress Cataloging in Publication Data

Lee, Jackson F.
    Providing for individual differences in student
learning.

    Bibliography: p.
    1. Competency based education. 2. Individualized
instruction. I. Pruitt, K. Wayne, II. Title. III. Title:
Mastery learning.
LC1031.L44 1984   371.3   84-2516
ISBN 0-398-05028-7

PREFACE

W ITH the recent emphasis on basic skills, many teachers, principals and curriculum specialists are searching for alternate ways to instruct the extremely diverse public school population. This book provides many ideas, strategies and suggestions which should prove beneficial in meeting some of the instructional needs of these key instructional personnel.

The general instructional approach advocated in this book is mastery learning. Mastery learning is a highly flexible system which considers student learning style, content difficulty, teaching style, and varying administrative philosophies. Specifically, this book describes a special brand of mastery learning, *Essentials-Correctives-Enrichment* (ECE), which is more adaptive in traditional school settings than other mastery learning systems. The ECE mastery model can be immediately plugged into existing school programs, whereas other mastery systems call for major system reforms with regard to time management, curriculum, grading approaches, and teaching strategies. Chapters One and Two detail the ECE model and elaborate on how this model differs from traditional instructional models and other mastery systems.

Subsequent chapters address objective writing skills, test construction, remediation techniques and enrichment activities. These instructional components are not unique to a mastery learning system. However, the way they are imbedded and utilized in the ECE model provides the instructional leader with a rather unique, sophisticated and systematic way to provide for differences in individual learners. Particular emphasis is placed on when to utilize large group and small group instruction, when and how to remediate, and providing enrichment which extends knowledge.

Practice exercises are provided after several skills sections in the book. The exercises are short and are included to give the reader a better grasp of the content contained in these key chapters. In addition, sample units are provided in the Appendix. One example written at the secondary level and one at the elementary level provide a good overview of the entire ECE model.

This book should be especially useful to classroom teachers, principals, and curriculum specialists who are seeking structured, yet flexible approaches to teaching any subject matter, particularly in basic skills areas. In addition, college instructors will find this book a valuable instructional manual in their elementary and secondary methods courses. Objective writing, test construction, and diagnostic/prescriptive teaching techniques are just a few of the topics usually covered in these pre-service and graduate level courses.

We have tried to sequence the book so that the introductory chapters give a broad overview of the ECE mastery model and subsequent chapters elaborate on specific components of the model found in the overview. The reader should read the book in its entirety, however, before attemtping to implement the suggestions found in the text. A casual perusal of the book might confuse rather than enlighten the reader.

While the content in the book is applicable to all educational levels from elementary school through college, the reader may find that the ECE model applies less advantageously to classes which are extremely homogeneous. Advanced academic courses and special education classes, for example, usually are made up of students who are on about the same academic level. In such cases, alternate instructional approaches to ECE should be utilized.

School personnel who have already used the ECE model have commented favorably on its logical structure, sound instructional principles and the positive effect it has on student learning. Students have even been reported making comments like, "I like it because my teacher is more organized", and "I like it because I know what is expected of me."

We like and endorse the system because we have observed many failing students meet success. This, in essence, is the goal of the book — to make all kids winners!

CONTENTS

PROVIDING
FOR INDIVIDUAL
DIFFERENCES
IN STUDENT LEARNING
A Mastery Learning Approach

Chapter 1
AN INTRODUCTION TO MASTERY LEARNING

Objectives: When you complete this chapter, you will be able to:
1. Define/describe five instructional variables in a mastery learning program.
2. Compare and contrast mastery learning with traditional approaches to instruction.

WHAT IS MASTERY LEARNING?

IN recent years, the increased amount of research on instruction has led many educators to attempt to apply some of the findings to schools in some systematic fashion. One such attempt is mastery learning, an approach to instruction which captilizes on the notion that almost all children can learn under certain prescribed conditions. The work of such noted educators as John Carroll and Benjamin Bloom has given credibility to the assumption that in fact almost all children can learn or master most of the content offered in our public schools.*

These prescribed conditions or variables as described by Bloom are necessary components of any instructional program which assumes accountability for student learning. Understanding these var-

---

*Bloom, Benjamin, "Learning for Mastery," *Evaluation Comment 1,* May, 1968.

iables is important to any person interested in utilizing a mastery learning approach to instruction. In the following pages, a thumbnail description is given of each variable.

1. Aptitude for Particular Kinds of Learning

It is a generally accepted fact that students have aptitudes for particular kinds of subjects. For example, some students are strong in math, while others might be strong in English or social studies. The fact that children are different and have different aptitudes is obvious even to the novice teacher. Many teachers believe, however, that students with a low aptitude are incapable of achieving at high levels. The working assumption of these teachers is that low aptitude equals low achievement and high aptitude equals high achievement.

Accepting this latter notion of aptitude runs counter to the position taken by John Carroll, who views aptitude as the amount of time required by the learner to attain mastery of a learning task.[*] This view suggests that in fact all children can learn at a very high level of proficiency if enough time is provided for mastery to take place. Thus, according to Carroll, a student with a high aptitude for a given subject would require less time to achieve mastery than one with a low aptitude for the same subject. Mastery learning, then, begins with the assumption that some provision must be made for the rates at which students learn.

2. Quality of Instruction

Traditionally, instruction has been defined in terms of group goals, materials and procedures. Schools themselves are also evaluated based on group achievement by grades or schools. Underlying this traditional view of public schooling is the assumption that all teachers teach alike and that all students learn alike.

If the quality of instruction is to improve and if student achievement levels are to increase, a new assumption must be introduced. This assumption is that individual students may need different types of instruction to attain mastery. Some students may require a tutor; others may require audio-visual presentations. Some students may

---

[*]Carroll, John B., "A Model of School Learning," *Teachers College Record*, 1963.

benefit from drill, recitation or lecture, while others may require something totally different.

The main thrust of this new assumption about instruction is that we must find out how a particular student learns and make every effort to provide that specific, individualized type of instruction if we expect the student to achieve at a maximum level.

3. Ability to Understand Instruction

When a student understands the details of a task, his or her responsibility in completing the task, and the level of mastery expected, chances are the task or goal will be attained more readily than when these aspects of instruction are unclear or vaguely stated by the teacher. Problems with clarity often result, for instance, when the same textbook is used with all students in a given classroom. Many textbooks are written with instructions and exercises for one level of students. When teachers rely on materials written on one level, they run the risk of confusing those students on levels other than the level utilized in a particular textbook.

While it is difficult for most teachers to individualize all lessons in all subjects, it is possible to modify instruction to increase a student's ability to understand instruction and achieve mastery. Small group instruction, audio-visual aids, tutorial assistance, performance objectives and other instructional variations are just a few of the devices available to teachers who want to individualize instruction in an effort to match student ability and level of instruction.

4. Perseverance

Teachers know that some students are willing to spend more time on some subjects than others. Usually, we explain this in terms of student interest or student abilities in the particular subject. If a student spends a lot of time drawing pictures we say that he likes art. He likes art because he is good in art or has an aptitude for art. Conversely, if another student spends little time drawing pictures, we are likely to say that he is not interested or has a low aptitude for art.

Teachers must find ways to encourage students to spend more time on subjects which usually cause them problems or for which they have low aptitudes. Instructional techniques such as emphasizing success rather than failure, teaching at an appropriate level, individualizing instruction, using positive reinforcement, giving immediate feedback of results and breaking learning into small, manageable steps all help increase the possibility that the student will succeed on a given unit of instruction. Success in one learning experience usually encourages the student to want to succeed. In this instance, success breeds perseverance which in turn produces further successes.

5. Time Allowed for Learning

If teachers can find ways to encourage students to persevere in difficult learning situations, the chances for student mastery are greatly improved. For mastery to take place on a large scale, however, adequate learning time must be made available. Increasing the availability to academic learning time can be a difficult task unless administrators and educators at all levels are willing to investigate alternate ways to administer school programs. Approaches which do not allow slower students more time for learning will have to be replaced by innovative approaches which allow students to progress at their own learning rates.*

MASTERY LEARNING AND TRADITIONAL INSTRUCTIONAL SYSTEMS

What, then, is mastery learning? Mastery learning is a flexible, adaptive approach to instruction in which individual learning styles and abilities are considered in the design of units of instruction. The chart on the next page contrasts traditional educational systems with mastery learning.

Bloom, pp.3-6

Contrasting Traditional Educational Systems
With Mastery Learning

Traditional	*Mastery of Learning*
1. large group instruction	1. individual, small group or large group instruction
2. content centered objectives	2. student centered objectives
3. passive student role	3. active student role
4. teacher role is one of disseminator of information	4. teacher role is one of manager of learning
5. students is accountable for achievement/success	5. student/teacher/system are accountable for achievement/success
6. evaluations usually limited to the determination of grades	6. evaluation is used to determine progress and final standing
7. grading is norm referenced	7. grading is criterion referenced
8. instruction is usually continuous i.e., when a student fails, he goes to a new unit of instruction	8. instruction is adaptable; when a student "fails", he is given another chance to succeed
9. teachers expect 1/3 of their students to fail	9. teachers expect most students to eventually "pass" their work
10. teacher uses one teaching strategy as a primary teaching mode	10. teacher uses a multi-faceted approach to teaching

The ten points of contrast under mastery learning incorporate the suggestions and ideas set forth by Bloom in the five variables of instruction which are covered in an earlier section of this chapter. The effective teacher might observe that mastery learning combines many of the instructional practices that he or she already employs. If this should be the case, the teacher is far ahead in understanding the general philosophy of mastery learning. Perhaps what makes this approach unique is the way these ideas are embodied in the instruction. Chapter Two describes one effective means by which mastery learning might be implemented.

Chapter 2

DESIGNING A MASTERY LEARNING MODEL

Objectives: When you have completed this chapter, you will be able to:
1. List and explain the components of a mastery learning approach.
2. List and explain the steps in implementing the ECE mastery learning model.

AFTER almost two decades of discussion and research regarding mastery learning, curriculum specialists have begun to evolve rather sophisticated instructional models for its implementation. Even a casual perusal of the literature in this area shows that most models contain the same basic components. Subtle changes regarding the use of particular types of objectives, evaluation procedures and the like may vary from school to school. In essence, however, the components noted below reflect what many feel to be the essential elements of any mastery learning model utilizing Blooms' five variables.

1. **Objectives:** These are the statements of learning outcomes which define mastery of a given unit of instruction. Usually, these are written in specific behavioral terms indicating what the learner will be able to do after instruction.

2. **Diagnostic Test:** A test often given prior to instruction which covers material found in all the unit objectives. The test is designed to determine prior knowledge of the content found in the unit objectives and/or the presence or absence of prerequisite skills.

3. **Instruction:** The teaching procedure used to teach the essential information, concepts, etc. contained in the objectives. Instruction is not limited to one way of teaching/learning. A wide variety of materials and flexible time frames which allow more learning time are important instructional considerations under a mastery learning system.

4. **Mastery Tests:** These tests are given at the end of the instructional phase. The score achieved on these tests determines whether a student has mastered the content.

5. **Remediation:** Remediation activities are designed for students who do not master the basic or minimum essentials as determined by the mastery tests.

STEPS IN PLANNING AND IMPLEMENTING THE ECE APPROACH TO MASTERY

The five components of mastery learning discussed in the preceding section give an overview of what is contained in any mastery system. Many variations or models exist which in one way or another utilize these components. The one described in this book is called the "Essentials, Correctives and Enrichment" model, hereafter referred to as ECE.

The ECE model is different from other mastery models in that it is easily adapted to existing school programs. For example, under the ECE model, schools do not necessarily have to abandon their grading, scheduling, and school grouping procedures. Under more individualized mastery models, these aspects of schooling must be revised if not abolished in order for the system to work proficiently. The steps summarized below show how a teacher might go about setting up a typical unit of instruction using the ECE model.

Phase I: Planning The Unit

Step 1: Select a Unit for Instruction

Units may vary in length from one to four or five weeks. However, it is best to make all units as short as possible. A two to four week unit is easier to manage. In the ECE model, the unit is divided into two parts. About one-half of the time allowed for the unit is spent in instruction of the Essential objectives and the remaining time spent in Enrichment and Correctives.

Step 2: Write objectives for all learning outcomes

These objectives should be stated in behavioral terms.

Step 3: Divide the Content and/or Skills into Two Groups

a. Essential objectives — These objectives represent those skills or content areas you feel are extremely important. To select these objectives, determine which skills, facts or concepts you feel to be absolutely essential for students in your class to master. Eliminate, for the time being, any of the "nice to know" material and focus on those minimum competencies students must have to function in and out of school. Express these minimum Essential competencies as behavioral objectives. Then, decide on what evidence you will accept as proof that students have mastered the objectives. (Chapter Three, "Writing Performance Objectives," will show the various ways this performance level can be stated.)

b. Enrichment — These objectives are important learning outcomes that, while significant, could be omitted by some students. Initially it might be helpful to list a few topics that you think might fall into this category. Later, you will be able to develop these topics. Also, keep in mind that your Essential objectives and Enrichment activities/objectives comprise the entire unit. The Enrichment phase is not a frills addition.

Step 4: Write a Test Question (Evaluation) for Each Essential Objective

Make sure that the test question matches the objective. (Chapter Five, "Measurement of Student Performance," will provide guidelines for writing good test items and matching the test items and the objective.)

Step 5: Develop a "Best Shot" Teaching Strategy for Each Essential Objective

This Best Shot teaching strategy should be the most effective method for a majority of the class members. A teacher's experience is usually reliable in helping to determine what methods do work and which ones do not. Large group instruction is acceptable at this point but small groups and individual instruction can be utilized. Some practice is advisable at this stage, but in most instances, practice should be kept at a minimum. (Chapter Seven, "Basic Instructional Principles," gives some useful teaching suggestions.)

Step 6: Write Correctives for Each Essential Objective

At this juncture, you are concerned with remediation of the Essential content. Variation of presentation is a main consideration. Although the number of Correctives may vary according to the difficulty of the objective, you should write about three Correctives for each objective. (Chapter Eight, "Providing Correctives," explains how to write and plan for Correctives.)

Step 7: Write Two Parallel Mastery Tests

a. Mastery Test I — Mastery Test I questions are taken directly from the objectives written for the Essential content covered under the Best Shot instruction.
b. Mastery Test II — This test is parallel to Mastery Test I in that it includes questions which are similar to but different in format from the test questions on Mastery Test I. The content covered by Mastery Test I and Mastery Test II is the same. It is administered after the student has finished his work on the Corrective track (Chapter Six, "Preparing Mastery Tests," shows how to write parallel tests.)

Step 8: Write Enrichment Objectives or Activities

In Step Two, you were asked to consider topics for Enrichment. Now, you need to formalize these objectives/activities. Remember, your Enrichment objectives/activities go beyond or extend the knowledge base of the Essential objectives. The means or standards by which you will measure "mastery" must be carefully specified at this point. Often, because of the nature of Enrichment objectives/activities, the use of percentages or other "hard" performance standards may not be practical. Checklists, observations and/or other evaluations are recommended. (Chapter Nine, "Providing Enrichment," provides direction for writing and implementing Enrichment activities/objectives.)

Step 9: Develop a grading policy

The final step in the planning phase is developing a comprehensive grading policy for your unit. One of the most crucial decisions will be choosing what score or evidence will indicate mastery based on your mastery test results. After the criteria for mastery have been selected, you will have to decide what letter grade will represent mastery. The grade of "C" is usually used in ECE. Another part of the policy will be to decide how much and what kinds of Enrichment activities will be required for grades of "A" and "B." (Chapters Eight through Eleven provide further insight into the development of a coherent grading policy.)

Phase Two: Implementation

Step 10: Present Instruction (Best Shot)

Teach the Essential objectives using the procedures you established in Step Four. Your instruction should take about one-half of the time allotted for your unit.

Step 11: Give Mastery Test I to All students

Mastery Test I is given after all of your Essential objectives have been taught. It is both a cumulative and formative examination. The score received on this test will determine if the student goes to the Corrective or Enrichment track.

Step 12: Provide Correctives and Enrichment

At this point, you present the Correctives you have prepared to all students who did not make the cutoff score on Mastery Test I. At the same time, students who did meet or excede the cutoff score on Mastery Test I should begin their Enrichment objectives/activities. Students will continue in these tracks until (1) Corrective students successfully complete Mastery Test II and begin Enrichment activities, (2) Enrichment students complete all activities required for an "A" or "B" (3) the next unit begins.

Step 13: Give Mastery Test II

Mastery Test II is a final or summative test given only to students on the Corrective track when they or the teacher feel they are ready. This may occur after one or more days of "Corrective instruction" or at the end of the time set aside for the unit. When a student masters or passes Mastery Test II, he or she should advance immediately to the Enrichment track and try to raise the C grade to either an A or B if time permits.

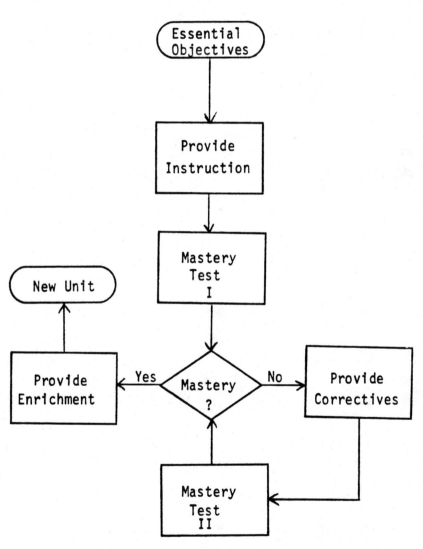

Figure 1. Implementing ECE

Step 14: Finish the Unit at the End of the Allotted Time

One of the features of ECE is that teachers are able to return to whole class instruction at the beginning of each new unit. Being able to "call time" at the end of a unit thus becomes a critical task. At this point the teacher has the option of terminating all activity on a set date or providing some overlap by allowing students to work on their own to complete Corrective or Enrichment activities. If the teacher decides to "close out" a unit, the student on the Corrective track has to take Mastery II and is awarded the grade received on that test. The student on the Enrichment track would receive the grade previously established for successful completion of a certain number of objectives/activities. Even if the teacher decides to extend the unit on an after-hours basis while a new unit is introduced, a stopping point has to be eventually established or bookeeping chores tie up the system. Whether a student should enter a new unit before the old unit is mastered is also a major consideration at this point. (Chapter Eleven, "Implementing ECE," will consider this or other points related to completing the unit.)

The fourteen steps in the ECE mastery model briefly explain the sequence which must be followed if mastery is to be attained by a large number of students. The sequence is less critical during the planning stage than during the implementation stage. It makes little difference, for example, if you plan the Best Shot teaching strategy before you write the test items or if you write Enrichment objectives or activities before you write Correctives. The steps outlined in this section provide a logical sequence for lesson plan development. (Appendix I and II provide sample lesson plans.) The steps (9-13) outlining implementation of the unit, however, should be followed as they are stated.

Chapter 3

WRITING PERFORMANCE OBJECTIVES

Objectives: When you complete this chapter, you will be able to:
1. Write original objectives which contain the three elements of a good performance objective.
2. Pick out poorly written objectives with regard to faulty criterion measures, performance behavior and conditions.
3. Rewrite poorly written objectives, replacing the faulty elements with correct ones.

PROPERLY stated objectives are essential to the teaching/ learning process. A good performance objective gives the teacher structure in organizing and presenting lessons as well as aiding in the preparation of tests which measure the skills/content dictated by the objective. For the student, a properly written objective indicates what and how well something is to be learned. It stands to reason that if a student fully understands what must be learned, the conditions for learning and the level of mastery expected for certain tasks, he/she will stand a better chance of mastery than if this information were not known.

ELEMENTS OF A PROPERLY STATED PERFORMANCE OBJECTIVE

The most generally accepted method for writing performance objectives is suggested by Robert F. Mager.* According to Mager, a properly stated objective should include three elements: (1) the specific behavior required of the student, (2) the conditions under which the student is going to be expected to perform this behavior and (3) the minimum level of student performance that will be considered as acceptable.

Consider the following objective: Given a new set of twenty miltiplication problems involving decimals, the student will correctly solve at least eighteen. In this objective, the three elements of a properly written objective are:

1. Do what? The student *will solve* simple multiplication problems involving decimals.
2. Under what conditions? Given a *new* set of twenty multiplication problems involving decimals.
3. How well? Eighteen of twenty must be correct.

Study the objectives below. Note the three elements of a properly written objective. The *what* element is underlined once, the *conditions* element twice, and the how well element is placed in parenthesis.

Samples of Properly Stated Objectives

1. The student will compare and contrast the main characters in two stories not read in class. (At least three points of comparison and two points of contrast must be given.)
2. The student will circle the main verb (in nine out of ten sentences) without the aid of a textbook.
3. After reading a new story, the student will list the main events of the story. (All the main events must be included and they must be in chronological order.)

After working through this chapter, you will be able to easily identify the three parts of a properly stated objective and write objectives which conform to the standards for good objective writing.

---

*Robert F. Mager: *Preparing Instructional Objectives,* Palo Alto: Fearon Publishers, 1962.

Do What?

In this section you will concentrate on the core element of a performance objective, the required behavior. For the time being, we will omit the conditions for performance and the minimum acceptable performance level elements of objectives. Remember that a performance objective should specify what a student will do or how he will act. The objectives will thus represent something observable. From the preceding examples, you might have noticed that the key element in any performance objective is the verb, specifically an action verb. Below are a few key verbs that indicate a clear performance or behavior.

Some Acceptable Behavioral Terms

Simple Tasks		More Complex Tasks	
add	identify*	appraise	paraphrase
arrange	label	argue	predict
calculate	locate	change	present
choose	mark	compare	propose
collect	match	defend	prove
count	organize	derive	rearrange
describe	outline	develop	reconstruct
document	select	estimate	rewrite
duplicate	translate	explain	signify
find	underline	formulate	structure

All of the verbs in this list are measureable or observable. Compare these to other verbs like know, understand, appreciate and review. The verbs in the latter group are vague and do not clearly show what the learner will be able to do after instruction. They require further elaboration. The verb "understand" for example, cannot be measured. On the other hand, "understanding" can be measured if by "understand" we mean outline, write, add, arrange or some other observable behavior.

Below are two objectives which contain the behavior only. Each

---

*Identify is an acceptable verb. However, in most instances, you will want to indicate the means of identification desired. Some means of identification are labeling, circling, underling, locating.

objective has been evaluated. Note the key questions with precede the evaluation.

Example 1: The Student Will Know the Eight Parts of Speech.

    a. *Does the objective state what the learner will be able to do after instruction?* Yes, but it is not an observable behavior.

    b. Is the behavior observable? No. How can a teacher (or anyone) *see* or measure knowing?

    c. *Is the verb a good one, ie., does it clearly show observable action?* No. It is an abstract verb.

Example 2: The Student Will Write in Order Each of the Letters of the Alphabet.

    a. *Does the objective state what the learner will be able to do after instruction?* Yes. He will write the alphabet.

    b. *Is the behavior observable?* Yes, writing can be seen.

    c. *Is the verb a good one?* Yes, writing is an action verb and easily observable.

Determining whether an objective contains a good *what* component can be confusing at first. We are so used to utilizing verbs like "understand," for example, that it is difficult at times to think divergently. The teacher usually knows what "understand" means in terms of instructional outcomes. The point is that in many instances, the teacher does not communicate that meaning to students, thus creating confusion over what is expected in the classroom. Continued practice with writing objectives which contain measurable, observable verbs usually eliminates most of the problems associated with the *what* aspect of the objective.

Exercise I
Behavioral and Non-behavioral Objectives

In each case below, indicate whether or not the objective has been stated in behavioral terms by writing "Yes" or "No" in the blank next to the number. Check your answers by using the key at the end of this chapter.

The Student Will:

——— 1. Appreciate World History.
——— 2. Write a well structured essay.
——— 3. Review the main idea(s) in "The Three Little Pigs."
——— 4. Understand a poem by T.S. Eliot.
——— 5. Build a bird house.
——— 6. Gain skill in the use of fractions.
——— 7. Compare and contrast the philosophies of Plato and Aristotle in an essay.
——— 8. Memorize the alphabet in order.
——— 9. Know the causes of the French Revolution.
——— 10. Recite the rule for adding fractions.

For further practice, write five objectives which contain clearly stated verbs. Then, have a friend check your work.

Conditions Stated in the Performance Objective

Once the desired behavior has been clearly stated, you have a solid base upon which to add the remaining two elements of a performance objective. The second element that will be considered is the statement of the conditions under which the student is expected to perform. This element is essential for resolving conflicts between teacher and student which stem from inadequate communication or hidden assumptions. Have you ever witnessed something like the following situations?

1. "But Mr. Jones, you said that we could use our calculators on this test! It's not fair to take them away now!"
2. "But Ms. Thompson, we have been practicing all week on how to look up words in the dictionary, but now you say we can't use it. Why?"
3. "Ms. Harris told us that the test would be on putting the capitals on a map of the states and now she asks us to draw the map, put in the states and then the capitals!! I wonder how she is going to like driving home on four flat tires?"

If these teachers had expressed the conditions for performance in advance, they might have avoided a lot of hard feelings and in one case, a long walk home.

Below are some samples of conditions of performance.

Conditions of Performance

Given a dead frog and a dissecting kit . . .
Given a list of 20 mispelled words . . .
Given the appropriate laboratory equipment . . .
Given a map of the states with the names of the states omitted . . .
Working alone and at home, each student will . . .
Working with members of his group, each student will . . .
During an oral presentation in front of the class . . .
Without the use of a pocket calculator . . .
Using only a dictionary . . .
Given a list of appropriate formulas . . .

Keep in mind that your objective represents what the student will be able to do after instruction. For this reason, it is rarely appropriate to use as conditions statements similar to the following:

> After reading and studying Unit III, the student will . . .

> After having been shown the proper use and care of painting equipment and having had proper practice in this area, the student will . . .

> After reading and discussing *The Naked Ape,* the student will . . .

These conditions are useless since we assume that the student will not be asked to demonstrate some new behavior until he has been given proper instruction. The conditions, then, should indicate those special circumstances under which the student will be asked to display his new behavior.

You may have noticed from the previous examples that there are several ways in which the conditions may be stated. You could indicate (1) what the student will be given, (2) what the student will be denied, or (3) the environment in which he must perform (in a group, alone, in public, in class, etc.). Study the three objectives below. The condition(s) of performance has been underlined:

Example 1: The Student Will List the Eight Parts of Speech.

The student will list *from memory* the eight parts of speech.

Example 2: *The Student Will Write the Alphabet. (Note the variations that are possible.)*

a. The student will write each letter of the alphabet *after the teacher calls out the letter.*

b. The student will write the alphabet *from memory on the chalkboard.*

c. The student will write the alphabet *in manuscript form on lined paper.*

Example 3: *The Student Will Run the Hundred Yard Dash.*

a. The student will run the hundred yard dash *without the use of starting blocks.*

b. The student will run the hundred yard dash *in a group of four students.*

Exercise II
Identifying Conditions of Performance

All of the objectives below have a condition(s) of performance. Underline the condition(s) in each objective and check your answers with the correct answers at the end of the chapter.

1. With the aid of a calculator, the student will multiply three digit numbers.
2. The student will recite the poem, "To A Daffodil," in front of the class without the use of notes.
3. The student will state three reasons for the fall of the Roman Empire. The textbook may be used.
4. The student will label the parts of a flower. He/she will be given a drawing of the flower and a scrambled list of flower parts.
5. Without the use of a globe or map, the student will draw an outline map of the North American continent.

For additional practice, add the *conditions* component to the five objectives you wrote under Exercise I. Again, have a friend check your work.

How Well? (Performance Levels)

Once you have designated what you want the student to do and the conditions under which you expect him to do it, you must then decide just how well he must perform to achieve mastery. The minimum level of acceptable performance must be precisely stated so that both the teacher and the student will know when the task has been successfully completed or the requirement met. Performance levels usually, but not necessarily, come at the end of the statement of an objective. The level may be expressed in any one of several ways. Study the examples below.

Ways of Expressing Performance Levels

1. The number of correct response out of so many
   . . . getting at least 8 out of 10 correct.
   . . . solving 2 out 3 division problems.
2. The percentage correct
   . . . defining at least 90 percent of the words correctly.
   . . . getting all of the easy problems correct and 50 percent of the difficult ones correct. (For young children not familiar with the concept of percentage, use 8 out of 10, 2 out of 3, 3 out of 4, etc. .)
3. The standards to be used in evaluating the behavior
   . . . with no spelling or major mechanical errors.
   . . . the essay must include at least five points of comparison between the two presidents.
   . . . the student's opinion must be substantiated by at least five facts and two expert opinions. All opinions should be attributed to the appropriate source.
4. The time allowed for completion
   . . . in forty-five minutes. Be careful using time as a performance level. Usually time is used in typing and physical education examples, but not in other instances.
5. 100 percent correct
   This level is implied when no other statement is given. WATCH OUT for those unstated assumptions, however; they could lead to that long walk home!

Study the examples below. Note the different ways of expressing performance levels. All performance levels are underlined with the exception of the implied 100 percent correct.

Example 1: The Student Will List the Eight Parts of Speech and *Correctly Label Each Part of Speech* in Sentences Prescribed by the Teacher.

(In this objective, 100 percent is implied.)

Example 2: The Student Will *List 7 out of 8* Parts of Speech.

(The number correct out of so many.)

Example 3: The Student Will Solve Previously Unencountered Linear Equations *Getting 100 percent of the Easy Problems and 50 Percent of the More Difficult Problems Correct.*

(The percentage correct.)

Example 4: The Student Will Write a Paragraph About His Favorite Winter *With No Spelling or Mechanical Errors.*

(Standards stated.)

Example 5: The Student Will Run the 100 Yard Dash in *14.5 Seconds or Less.*

(Time allowed.)

Exercise III
Identifying Performance Levels

Underline the performance level in each of the objectives below. If a performance level is implied, place an "I" at the end of the objective. Check your answers with the key at the end of the chapter.

1. The student will add seven out ten (7/10) two digit numbers.
2. The student will describe without the aid of a textbook the main character in "The Little Blue House." At least seven statements of description must be included.
3. The student will rewrite a paragraph consisting of ten double negatives, changing the double negatives to their proper forms. (8/10)

4. The student will compare and contrast the French Revolution and the American Revolution, giving at least five points of comparison and five points of contrast.
5. When shown flash cards containing "sight words," the student will correctly pronounce (say) fifteen out of twenty words.

For further practice, add the performance level to the five objectives you have already written. Have a friend check your work. You should have written five complete behavioral or performance objectives.

A FINAL NOTE ON WRITING PERFORMANCE OBJECTIVES

Writing clearly stated behavioral or performance objectives can be a tedious task at first. As you practice writing more objectives, the process becomes easier. As you write or revise objectives from year to year, you will eventually settle on the exact conditions, performance levels, and verbs that have meaning for students. Once the good, descriptive verb has been found for a particular learning task, you will find that this verb is useable year after year. On the other hand, different conditions and performance levels may be required for different groups of students. Varying performance levels and conditions are instructional decisions and should not alter the style in which the objectives are written.

ANSWERS TO EXERCISES

Exercise I: Behavioral and Non-Behavioral Objectives.

No   1. (Can you measure *appreciate?*)
YES   2. (*Write* is observable)
NO   3. *Review* is too abstract and broad)
NO   4. (How do you measure *understanding?*)
YES   5. (*Build* is observable)
NO   6. (*Gain skill* is too broad)
YES   7. (Both *verbs* are observable)
NO   8. (*Memorize* is a mental activity)

NO 9. (How do you measure *know?*)
YES 10. (*Recite* is observable/measureable)

Exercise II: Identifying Conditions for Performance.

1. *With the aid of a calculator,* the student multiply three digit numbers.
2. The student will recite the poem, "To A Daffodil," *in front of the class and without notes.*
3. The student will state three reasons for the fall of the Roman Empire. *The textbook may be used.* (Note that conditions do not have to be imbedded in the main clause.)
4. The student will label the parts of a flower. *He will be given a drawing of the flower and a scrambled list of flower parts.*
5. *Without the use of a globe or map,* the student will draw an outline map of the North American continent.

Exercise III: Identifying Performance Levels.

1. The student will add *7/10* two digit numbers.
2. The student will describe without the aid of a textbook the main characters in "The Little Blue House." *At least seven statements of description must be included.*
3. The student will rewrite a paragraph consisting of ten double negatives, changing the double negatives to their proper forms. *(8/10)*
4. The student will compare and contrast the French Revolution and the American Revolution, *giving at least five points of comparison and five points of contrast.*
5. When shown flash cards containing "sight words," the student will correctly pronounce (say) *fifteen out of twenty words.*

Chapter 4

ORDERING AND SELECTING OBJECTIVES

Objectives: When you complete this chapter, you will be able to:
1. Identify objectives written at the three taxonomic domains.
2. Identify objectives at the three levels in the cognitive domain.
3. Raise lower level objectives to higher level objectives in the cognitive domain.

M OST teachers know the basic objectives they need to teach. However, teachers need to know how to raise or lower the level of their objectives to accomodate learning style, ability levels and rates of learning. They also need to know how to select and write objectives which might be considered either essential or "nice-to-know" information. These considerations are vitally important in light of basic skills developments in most states.

TAXONOMIC DOMAINS

Bloom's taxonomy of educational objectives describes three different categories or domains of learning behaviors.* These three domains are described as follows.

---

*Benjamin Bloom, Engelhart, *et. al.*, *Taxonomy of Educational Objectives*, Handbook I: Cognitive Domain, New York: David McKay Company, 1974.

The Three Domains in the Taxonomy

Cognitive Domain:

This domain is concerned with intellectual skills such as remembering and problem solving. Most formal school activities are at least outwardly cognitive in nature.

Affective Domain:

This domain is concerned with such aspects as interests, values, feelings, and attitudes.

Psychomotor Domain:

This domain is concerned with physical abilities such as shooting a basketball, knitting, typing and penmanship.

Since these three domains are really part of an artificial system i.e., one that was man-made to classify situations that would otherwise be unclassifiable, the domains are rarely completely separate from each other. In fact, all three domains are usually present to some degree in any learning situation. The domain in which an objective should be classified, then, depends on the teacher's goal. If, for instance, you asked your class to write a theme on "My Summer Vacation," it could be classified in several ways:

Cognitive: If you were concerned about a student's skill in communication and/or self-expression.

Affective: If you were looking for indications of what activities interested the students so that you could include them in instruction.

Psychomotor: If you were concerned with whether or not the student could write legibly.

EXERCISE I
Identifying Domains

Following is a list of objectives which contain behaviors that might be found in instructional situations. On the blank to the left of each number, indicate the domain in which the statement should be classified, using the following code: (C)-Cognitive; (A)-Affective; (P)-Psychomotor. The answers are at the end of the chapter.

_____ 1. The student will voluntarily attend three concerts this year.

_____ 2. The student will list, on his own, all the books he has read this summer.

_____ 3. The student will be able to throw a ten yard spiral pass with a football.

_____ 4. The student will list the eight parts of speech.

_____ 5. The student will recite the Gettysburg Address.

_____ 6. The student will purchase his own set of paints at home without being asked to do so.

_____ 7. The student will make a leather belt.

_____ 8. The student will defend his answer with four examples from his reading.

_____ 9. The student will list, in order, the notes which go in the spaces of a musical staff.

_____ 10. Using the standards of criticism studied in this class, the student will write a two-page essay on the elements of style in Hemingway's short story, "The Killers."

Since most teachers are more involed in writing objectives in the cognitive domain, the emphasis in the remainder of the chapter will be on understanding and analyzing aspects of the cognitive domain.

Levels in the Cognitive Domain

The cognitive domain is divided into six levels. These levels are listed in order of increasing complexity and difficulty of the intellectual task required, ranging from the ability to memorize to the ability to make abstract evaluations. Although the levels are given as being discrete classifications, it should be noted that some overlap usually exists. Where overlap exists, a teacher must use his best judgement as to where a task should be classified. To simplify your task of learning to use the taxonomy, we have grouped Bloom's six levels into three broader levels. These are described below.

Levels in the Cognitive Domain

Level I: *Memory*
    1. Knowledge

Level II: *Simple Understanding*
     2. Comprehension
     3. Application
Level III: *Complex Understanding*
     4. Analysis
     5. Synthesis
     6. Evaluation

In the following sections, explanations of these six sub-levels will be given. Because these six sub-levels are so narrowly defined and discrimination often difficult to make, you only need to know how to classify objectives at each of the three main levels, coded above as Level I, Level II, and Level III.

EXPLANATION OF LEVELS IN THE COGNITIVE DOMAIN

Level I: Memory

(1) Knowledge — This lowest cognitive level is concerned with a student's ability to memorize. This memorization can be as short as the repeating of significant historical dates (When did Columbus discover America?) or as long as duplication from memory of complex patterns e.g., (1) draw the Krebs cycle from memory or (2) list in order all the steps necessary to make a bill into a law.

Much of what students learn in school could be classified at the knowledge level. Teachers who feel that they are teaching their students to think often give test items like "trace the course of events which led up to the starting of the Civil War." More often than not, however, this material was covered the day before in class and the student is required to do little more than repeat exactly what the teacher said. Thus, the task, rather than requiring thinking, requires only the ability to memorize.

Level II: Simple Understanding

(2) Comprehension — This is the lowest level of what can be called understanding. Here a student must use his "knowledge" and change it in some simple way to indicate that its meaning has been grasped. "Comprehension" and "Knowledge" constitute the vast majority of academic tasks. Several sub-categories exist which might aid you in learning to write objectives at the comprehension level. These sub-categories, which are given below, are presented here only for the purpose of clarification.

    a. Translation — Students who are asked to translate are required to change a communication (words or symbols) into some other form of communication. Asking a student to write a definition of "government" in his own terms, for example, calls for a translation. Converting word problems into mathematical formulas would be another task requiring translation.

    b. Interpretation — Students who interpret material must either summarize it or change it around to show understanding of the material. Writing a summary of a short story or paraphrasing a particular argument are examples of interpretaion tasks.

    c. Extrapolation — If you were given a graph which showed a definite trend and were asked to predict from the graph whether this trend would continue, that would be an extrapolation task. In extrapolation the student is given some concrete materal (chart, graphs, description) and is asked to predict from that material.

(3) Application — At this level the student has to memorize the material and grasp the meaning of it and decide *when* the material is useful. With "comprehension" the student is given concrete material to respond to and is given procedural directions, e.g., "solve the following problem using the quadratic formula, or use the dictionary to define these words . . . " With "application", on the other hand, the student is given a problem or situation that is new and must then decide which of the principles, concepts, methods, laws, or theories that have been learned might be used to solve the problem. Note also that just because a test objective or item says "apply" does not mean that it calls for abilities at the application level. "Apply the quadratic equation to the following problem" is a comprehension level task.

The main differences between the comprehension and application levels, then, are that:

- At the application level students are given unique and somewhat abstract material to respond to, whereas the comprehension level uses more familiar and concrete material.
- At the comprehension level, students are given clues and direc-

tions as how to solve a given problem; at the application level, students are given a minumum amount of direction.

Because the differences between the two categories are often difficult to discern, you will find it helpful to group both comprehension and application level tasks into Level II: Simple Understanding.

Level III: Complex Understanding

For a student to perform on Level III, he/she must have mastered the content at Levels I and II and then go beyond to more abstract uses. Level III is seldom applicable to students below the fourth grade. Older students, however, need practice in higher level intellectual skills to function more effeciently in everyday life. Unfortunately, students are given too little practice in this area.

(4) Analysis — This requires more understanding than is necessary at Level II. Not only does the student have to identify the parts of a given communication (comprehension) but he has to explain the relationship between those parts. At the analysis level, the student is looking for abstract relationships and structures. The following examples indicate analysis level tasks:

a. Given a T.V. commercial, the student will record all major statements and indicate whether they are based on fact or opinion.

b. Given a political argument, the student will identify the unstated assumptions which underlie the argument.

c. Given a case study, the student will outline the problem and its major components.

d. Given a poem by T.S. Eliot, the student will describe those characteristics of style which are unique to that poet.

(5) Synthesis — Synthesis tasks require the student to produce something new or original. The word "creativity" is strongly related to synthesis behaviors. It is generally assumed, however, that the unique behavior required by a synsthesis task has some underlying intellectual skills at Levels I and II. Although a chimpanzee can paint abstract art, the task itself (although possibly not the painting) will be very different if done by a trained artist who is painting to express a certain idea or feeling. It is difficult to identify synthesis behaviors since something which appears to be a unique production of the student may really be just a copy of one previously learned. The following tasks might represent behaviors at the synthesis level:

a. Write a new poem in the Shakespearian style.
b. Design a new experiment to demonstrate Archimedes' principle.
c. Paint a landscape using only blues and greens.
d. Given a description of an unstable political situation, describe how you could set up your own provisional government.

Notice that in example "b" the experiment only has to be *unique for the student*. Whether his unique experiment was done two hundred ago does not really matter as long as it is new to him. In this sense, he "created" it. If in example "d" the student takes a set governmental pattern (e.g., dictatorship) and just describes it, then the task is really one of comprehension (or at best application) since the student has not created anything.

(6) Evaluation — The evaluation tasks requires skills or behaviors taken from all the previous categories. To evaluate a situation, a student must place a judgement on a situation or production and then back up his judgement. The judgement may be based on one of two criteria. Some situations or works must be judged on the basis of *internal* evidence. This evidence can be such things as accuracy, validity, adherence to rules of logic, or the consistency of the argument. The following examples require the student to evaluate on the basis of internal evidence:

a. Which of the following two reports most accurately describes what happened in the assembly yesterday? Defend your answer.
b. Given a new play by Eugene O'Neill, the student will evaluate it (decide on its worth) using the following criteria . . . .

One can also judge something on the basis of *external* evidence. This "outside" evidence could be such things as comparison with other works in the field, the relationship between ends versus means, utility, or efficiency. The following examples require the student to evaluate on the basis of external evidence:

a. Given descriptions of the four current leading health care proposals, decide which should be selected on the basis of the cost/efficiency relationship of each proposal. Defend your selection.
b. Is *Gulag Archepelago* a significant literary work? Defend your

answer.

c. Is the student council in our school functioning at its maximum efficiency? What could be done to improve it if it needs improving? Defend your answer.

Keep in mind that although each of the three Levels is thoroughly explained in this chapter, you should only concentrate on the broad classifications. In the following exercise, you are asked to classify each objective into one of the three broad Levels. In the answer key, however, sub-levels as well as levels are given. This is done merely as follow-up and practice for what has been covered so far in this chapter.

Exercise II: Identifying Level I, II, and III Objectives

For each of the following objectives, indicate whether it belongs on Level I, II, or III by so marking in the blank in front of the number. Check your answers with the answers at the end of the chapter.

_____ 1. The student will design an original experiment to prove or disprove the hypothesis that "girls learn faster than boys."

_____ 2. Given a set of unknown rocks, the student will be able to select those which are metamorphic.

_____ 3. Given a new painting, the student will critique it on the basis of its ability to express (via appropriate technique) the painter's stated purpose.

_____ 4. The student will design and draw his own campaign poster in support of a local candidate of his choice.

_____ 5. The student will write a good definition of "stratosphere" in his own words.

_____ 6. Given a scrambled list of the categories in the *Taxonomy of Educational Objectives,* the student will arrange these in proper order.

_____ 7. The student will write the definition of "irony" in his own words.

_____ 8. The student will compose a simple one line melody.

_____ 9. Given a description of a person and a joke told by that person, the student will describe what the joke tells about that person's personality.

_____ 10. Given the first four lines of a poem, the student will complete the poem in no less than eight additional lines using the same style, moode, and content.

_____ 11. The student will state at which level in the cognitive domain the following behavioral objectives have been written . . . .

_____ 12. After viewing the films on both rich and impoverished families, the student will describe the disadvantages of being in either group.

_____ 13. The student will write from memory the definition of photosynthesis.

_____ 14. The student will list the eight parts of speech.

_____ 15. The student will compare and contrast art in the Renaissance with art in the Middle Ages.

RAISING OBJECTIVES IN THE COGNITIVE DOMAIN TO HIGHER LEVELS

Too often the objectives used by teachers, whether stated or unstated, focus on learning at the knowledge level. This fact is true in part because (1) it is easier to prepare objectives and teach at this level, (2) most teachers have been taught by teachers who have placed strong emphasis on memory tasks, and (3) since few students master thinking skills, it is often frustrating for both teacher and student when a teacher requires mastery of higher level skills.

One of the best ways to remember a principle, rule, concept or fact is to use it in some meaningful situation. Observe the two objectives and determine which one is more meaningful.

1. The student will list the name and distinguishing characteristics of each phylum in the animal kingdom.
2. Given an unknown live or preserved animal specimen, the student will classify it in the correct phylum.

In the second objective, the student has to memorize the names and characteristics of each phyla and use this information to classify animals. Not only would the skill indicated by the second objective be more interesting to learn and demonstrate, but the student would also retain the names and characteristics longer. We say that objective two is written at a higher level.

Listed below are two more examples of objectives which have been raised to higher levels. Study these two examples and note how the tasks are similar and different:

Example 1:

Objective:The student will list all the steps required for the preparation of sulfur dioxide.

Revision: The student will prepare sulfur dioxide.

Example 2:

Objective: The student will define the word "sentence" as "a group of words having a subject and verb and makes sense."

Revision: a. Write two sentences which meet our definition of a sentence.

b. Given a list of sentences and meaningless word groups, the student will select those word groups that are sentences.

In both revisions, the student is asked to exercise more understanding than is required for mere recall or memorization of facts. He is asked to apply or use knowledge.

RELATING THE TAXONOMY TO ECE

Raising objectives to a higher level is an easy task if the teacher is familiar with the taxonomy of educational objectives discussed in this chapter. Many teachers do not practice this skill because under traditional systems, the need does not exist to revise the original set of objectives.

Under the ECE mastery system, the teacher is almost forced to raise the level of objectives as he or she prepares the objectives for the Essential and Enrichment phases of instruction. Most Essential objectives will probably be Level I and Level II objectives. Level III objectives are usually placed in the Enrichment Phase. Which objectives are placed in the Essential or Enrichment track, however, is an instructional decision that only the teacher can make.

In determining whether an objective should be utilized at the Essential or Enrichment phase, the teacher has to first determine what will be accepted as minimum requirements for passing and then raise the level of the objective to a Level II or III objective. In classes with slower students, Level II objectives may in fact constitute the Enrichment phase of instruction. In more advanced classes, Level III objectives are utilized in most cases in the Enrichment Phase of instruction.

Some objectives written at Level II, then, may be used at the Essential or Enrichment phase of instruction. A teacher should not make the assumption, however, that slow students can function only at Level I. Under the ECE System, many students master objectives at higher levels because of the corrective analysis and remediation procedures built into the system. Students should always be encouraged to go beyond the minimum Essentials to the more challenging and, in many cases, more enjoyable, Enrichment objectives.

ANSWERS TO EXERCISES

Exercises I: Identifying Domains.

A	1.	A	2.	P	3.	C	10.
C	4.	C	5.	A	6.		
P	7.	C	8.	C	9.		

Exercise II: Identifying level I, II and III Objectives.

1. III (Synthesis)	6. II (Comprehension)	11. II (Comp. or App.)
2. II (Application)	7. II (Comprehension)	12. III (Evaluation)
3. III (Evaluation)	8. III (Synthesis)	13. I (Knowledge)
4. III (Synthesis)	9. III (Evaluation)	14. I (Knowledge)
5. II (Comprehension)	10. III or II	15. III (Analysis)

Chapter 5

MEASUREMENT OF STUDENT
PERFORMANCE

Objectives: When you complete this chapter, you will be able to:
1. Evaluate the quality of test items by comparing sample items which objectives and basic rules for item writing.
2. Write test items, check lists and rating scales which match objectives and which conform to the rules for writing these measurement devices.

E VEN the best instructional planning and methodologies can be negated by the use of faulty measurement procedures. This chapter will provide a brief review of some of the essential rules of classroom measurement and item writing, the ones that most frequently cause trouble. More in depth information on the subject of item writing can be found in any of the current texts in testing and measurement.

GENERAL GUIDELINES FOR CLASSROOM MEASUREMENT

- Write specific behavioral objectives for all learning outcomes. The preparation of specific objectives prior to instruction is one of the cornerstones of any mastery learning strategy. These objectives will dictate the type of test items used and the content of those items.

- Develop an evaluation plan and evaluation instruments prior to instruction. In ECE several opportunities for measurement must be anticipated. Students will have to be evaluated on:
  - practice exercises during instruction
  - Mastery Tests I and II
  - each Corrective activity
  - each Enrichment activity

It might be noted that diagnostic testing is excluded from the list above. Remember that while this type of testing is effective and certainly not inconsistent with ECE, its presence has been sacrificed in an effort to provide an opportunity for large group instruction at the beginning of each unit.

- Test items or other assessment devices should match stated objectives. This content validity is another essential element of mastery learning. To insure objective/item correspondence, two suggestions might prove useful:

  - Where relatively few objectives are being presented, each objective should be measured. Where a large number of independent objectives are being covered, care must be taken to insure that a representative sample of the objectives is measured.
  - The test should match objectives in both type of task and level of difficulty. If, for instance, your objective calls for students to be able to *list and describe* the steps in a particular sequence, then your test item should call for the student to *list and describe* these steps.

Try the following exercise to get a better feel of how objectives and items should match.

EXERCISE I
Matching Objectives and Test Items

Directions: Match each objective in the left-hand column with the test item that measures it from the right-hand column. Each test item may be used once, more then once or not at all. The answers will be found at the end of the chapter.

Objectives

_____ 1. Given a list of the names of organisms, the student will circle examples of fungi.

_____ 2. The student will write the defintion of fungi.

_____ 3. Given a list of fungi, the student will describe where each may be found.

_____ 4. Given a list of definitions of plant groups, the student will identify the one for fungi.

_____ 5. Given pictures or drawings of various organisms, the student will mark those showing fungi.

_____ 6. The student will list the names of three common fungi.

Test Items

a. Circle the definition for fungi:
   a. an organism having true leaves and a stem
   b. a non-green plant reproducing by spores
   c. one-celled aquatic plants
   d. a non-green plant which has a flower

b. Define fungi: _____

c. On pictures or drawings above, place an X on all those which are examples of fungi.

d. Where might you locate each of the following fungi:
   a. Shelf fungi _____
   b. Athlete's foot _____
   c. Toadstools _____

e. Circle any organism below which is a fungus:
   Pine tree   Mold   Bacteria
   Mushroom Indian Pipe Protococcus

f. What is a fungus? _____
   _____

g. Write the names of three common fungi:
   1. _____
   2. _____
   3. _____

h. A fungus reproduces by means of
   a. seeds
   b. cones
   c. spores
   d. spontaneous generation

- **Follow-up each test carefully.** This follow-up should include:
    1. Providing some form of feedback to the student within one hour of the test. The test need not be graded at this time (such would be physically impossible in most cases), but you can share a list of correct answers, sample items or grading criteria immediately after the test.
    2. Writing comments on each test. Comments should include constructive criticism and encouragement.
    3. Grading each test item and revising and/or replacing faulty ones.

GUIDELINES FOR ITEM WRITING

In addition to conforming to the measurement principles provided above, teachers must strive to insure that all test items are well written. The suggestions provided below should serve as a brief review of a few of the most frequently abused principles.

Essay Items

- Be sure the question or task is clear to the student. Include some mention of the criteria to be used for evaluation in the item itself. For more elaborate written work, such as reports or projects, a criterion checklist or sample of the finished product is often helpful in clarifying the task.
- Do not use essays to measure knowledge or memory level skills or content.
- Do not permit students a choice of questions unless they are to select from options which will permit each test to be of equal difficulty. In the examples below, notice that in the first case grades could be influenced by the difficulty of the items chosen. In the second example, giving students an option of which battle to describe should keep the tests more or less equivalent.

Example 1 (weak):

Directions: Choose any three of the items below and answer them using complete sentences.

1. Describe the key events in the Battle of Gettysburg. Be sure to indicate the generals for both sides, the victor and the strategy used by the victor.
2. List the 5 major causes of the Civil War.
3. Describe the two major factors leading to the South's defeat.
4. Describe how the personality and background of Grant differed from that of Lee.

Example 2 (Improved):

Directions: Answer each of the items given below in complete sentences.
1. Choose any battle listed below and describe it in a paragraph. Be sure to indicate the generals for both sides, the victor and the strategy used by the victor.
   a. Gettysburg
   b. Bull run
   c. Chancellorsville
2. List the 5 major causes of the Civil War.
3. Describe the two major factors leading to the South's defeat.
4. Describe how the personality and background of Grant differed from that of Lee.

- Be sure to give students adequate time to answer each question. The longer the response required, the fewer items that should be given on the test.
- For long essays, prepare a checklist or rating scale to guide in scoring. For shorter essays, a model answer can be used for scoring.
- Evaluate each student's answer to one item before going on to the next item. This practice will improve the fairness of the scoring.

Short Answer, Completion or Fill-In-The-Blanks

- Use this item format whenever you wish to measure a student's ability to *recall* information as opposed to his being able to *recognize* or *select* information.
- Whenever possible, state the item as a direct question. In most cases, this type of question will be clearer to the student. Read the two items that follow to see the difference between the direct ques-

tion in the second example and an ambiguous fill-in-the-blank item in the first. Notice that the first example could be answered by such undesired but true responses as "a general," "a Virginian," or "a man with wooden teeth."

The father of our country was _____

Who was the father of our country?_____

- State the item so that only a single brief answer is possible. Using direct questions will often take care of this rule. If you feel that leaving a blank in a sentence will improve communication, however, make sure the intended answer is clearly best. Compare the two examples below and notice how the second is clearer than the first.

Richard Nixon was _____

The highest political office held by Richard Nixon was _____

- State the item so that the blank will come at the end of the item.
- For mathematics problems, consider giving credit for both the product (answer) and the process (means of arriving at the answer) when evaluating responses.
- Do not lift a passage from a source and leave several words blank. These items often lack sufficient cues to provide a meaningful task. The passage below provides an example of a chopped-up passage. Notice that it does not present a clear task for the student.

The __1__ __2__ is often __3__ except when the __4__ __5__ is on the __6__ .

Multiple Choice

- The stem or question part of the item should present a clear problem, statement or task. As with short answer items, a direct question is often the most simple straightforward approach. One quick way to test the quality of a stem is to hide the alternatives (the choices) and see if the question could be answered as a short answer item. If it can be answered as a short answer item, it is probably a clear task. Compare the two stems which follow. Notice that the first does not present any kind of meaningufl task. The second, however, is so clear that it could be answered without using alternatives.

Abraham Lincoln wrote:
In which of the following documents did Abraham Lincoln formally free the slaves?

- Avoid the use of negative items. Item stems such as "Which of the following is *NOT* a stage in mitosis?" rarely measure significant learning. Why is it important to know what is *not* a stage? In some cases where you want students to know what is *not* true or what to avoid, negative items can be used. You may, for example, wish to emphasize the danger of moving persons suspected of having neck injuries by asking the question "Which of the following actions should be *AVOIDED* when treating an accident victim suspected of having neck injuries?" If negative wording is used, make sure that it is emphasized by capitalization, italics and/or underlining.
- Make all of the alternatives plausible. Putting in alternatives that are absurd may improve grades but they reduce the ability of the item to separate those who know the information from those who do not.
- Avoid the use of "all of the above" and "none of the above" as alternatives. The use of these alternatives is not wrong but is often leads to problems such as logical inconsistencies or clues to the answer.

MATCHING

A matching item should be used only when each item in the right hand column is a reasonable guess for each item in the left hand column. For example:

If this column contains	*Then this should contain*
inventions	inventors
book titles	authors
poems	poets
historical events	dates
definitions	words
organisms	phyla
important quotations	writers

Use an item format which will effectively measure a student's knowledge without being confusing. The example below provides a model of an effective item along with a set of complete instructions.

Directions: The column on the left contains a list of chemical elements. On the blank in front of each element, place the letter of its symbol from the column on the right. Each symbol may be used once, more than once, or not at all.

Element	*Symbol*
_____ 1. Iron	a. P
_____ 2. Potassium	b. Ph
_____ 3. Phosphorus	c. I
_____ 4. Gold	d. K
_____ 5. Silver	e. Ag
	f. Au
	g. G
	h. Fe

- Do not have an even match of items from the two columns.
- Keep the columns short — about fifteen items as a maximum. If you have a large amount of homogeneous material to test, use several matching items. Put the longest material in the left-hand column. This position makes answering easier and faster for most students.

Alternative Response/True-False

- Use alternative response/true-false items whenever two choices are available. Don't feel limited to the traditional true-false type questions. Items calling for answers such as yes-no or fact-opinion can be very useful.
- Keep each item short and simple. Include only one important idea in each statement.
- Avoid negative statements. Negative statements often lead to confusion and spurious responses. The first two items that follow are more confusing than if they were expressed in positive form. Notice how much easier the revised versions are.

Poor Items:

Richard Nixon was *not* a Democrat.
No, turtles are *not* reptiles.

Improved:

Richard Nixon was a Democrat.
Turtles are reptiles.

- Remember that statements of opinion cannot be true or false, thus they must be attributed to some source.
5. Use a large number of items to insure test reliability.

Checklists and Rating Scales

Often a test is an inappropriate technique for evaluating an objective. In such cases, the use of a checklist or rating scale can increase the reliability of your evaluation.

Checklists:

Checklists are used when you need to evaluate only the presence or absence of a particular trait or set of traits. The list of traits should include those behaviors or characteristics that must be noted. Common errors may also be added to the list. The example below shows how a simple checklist is used to evaluate an otherwise untestable objective:

Objective: The student will develop and produce a campaign poster for the presidential candidate of his or her choice. The poster should include appropriate use of at least one standard advertising device, color and clarity of message.

Student Checklist

_____ 1. The poster is neatly produced.
_____ 2. Color is used effectively to gain attention and/or give a message.
_____ 3. At least one standard advertising device is employed.
_____ 4. The message of the poster is clear.

Rating Scales: Rating scales are used to evaluate the degree to which a behavior or characteristic is present. Such a scale will usually contain a list of essential characteristics along with some numerical, graphic or descriptive scale. The sample below uses a numerical scale to rate the campaign poster required by the objective given above.

Criteria	Poor	Marginal	Adequate	Very Good
Neatness	1	2	3	4
Use of Color	1	2	3	4
Use of Advertising device	1	2	3	4
Clarity	1	2	3	4

In this chapter, you have only been exposed to the highlights of testing and measurement concepts and techniques. You should have enough information, however, to help you avoid some of the common mistakes that undermine otherwise exemplary teaching efforts. Before leaving this chapter, you may wish to complete Exercise 2 which asks you to evaluate and correct some faulty items.

EXERCISE 2

Identifying and Correcting Defective Test Items

Directions: For each item below, (1) indicate the main fault or faults and (2) revise the item or describe how it could be repaired.

A. Essay Item
   Comment on "Custer's Last Stand."
B. Completion and Short Answer Items
   a. The President of the United States Is _____.
   b. There are many kinds of _____.
   c. _____ is the Capital of Virginia.
C. Multiple Choice Items
   1. Which of the following towns is *not* in South Carolina?
      a. Florence   c. Columbia
      b. Raleigh   d. Ninety-six
   2. What is the state bird of South Carolina?
      a. Gnat   c. Dogwood
      b. Carolina Wren   d. Robin

3. George Washington
   a. Was the father of our country.
   b. Hated cherries.
   c. Was toilet trained late in life.
   d. Loved to stand in boats.
D. True-False Items
   1. Four is not the product of three times one.   T or F
   2. All citizens should be permitted to vote.   T or F
   3. Music is enjoyed all over the World.
      In the U.S., however, the most popular
      form of music is rock.   T or F
E. Matching Items
   Directions: Match these questions:
   a. West Indies   _____ 1. The man who dis-
                                          covered America in
                                          1492.

   b. *Santa Maria*   _____ 2. The date America
                                          was discovered.

   c. Christopher Columbus   _____ 3. One of the boats
                                          used to discover
                                          America.

   d. *Nina*   _____ 4. Another of the boats
                                          used to discover
                                          America.

   e. 1492

ANSWERS TO EXERCISES

Exercise 1: Matching Objectives and Test Items.

1. e
2. b (f is a poor choice because the question is vague).
3. d
4. a
5. c
6. g

Exercise 2: Identifying and Correcting Defective Test Items.

A. This task is too broad. There are no limits to the type or length of desired students responses. A simple revision might be "List and describe the five events which led to the defeat of General Custer at the battle of the Little Big Horn."

B. 1. The task is unclear. Answers could vary from the name of the current President to "elected every four years." Why not use a direct question such as "Who is the current President of the United States?"

   2. No clear question is presented. Many teachers write this type of item expecting students to memorize the answers to poorly worded questions. How useful is such an accomplishment?

   3. The blank should come at the end of the item. An improved form would be, "What is the name of the Capital city of Virginia?"

C. 1. Why is the item negative? Who cares what town is *not* in South Carolina? The item stem should be stated in a positive form such as "Which town is in eastern South Carolina?"

   2. Although many of the residents of the Palmetto State might be tempted to select option a, the only reasonable choices are b and d. All alternatives should be plausible. Change options a and d to names of local birds.

   3. The stem does not present a clear task (try covering the alternatives). Also, the wrong answers are not plausible. Almost any revision of this item will be an improvement.

D. 1. This is a negative item. Also, if we are interested in determining the student's ability to multiply 4 X 3, then this should be a short answer or a multiple choice item.

   2. This statement is an opinion and thus should not be used as a true-false item. The item could be improved by ascribing this opinion to some famous individual such as Thomas Jefferson or Susan B. Anthony.

   3. Too many separate ideas are contained in this item. A revision might be, "More rock albums are sold each year than any other single type of music."

E. Many parts of this item need to be repaired.

   1. The material is not homogeneous. The list contains ships, a location, a date and a name.

2. The directions are useless as they are stated.
3. The long material should be in the left-hand column along with the numbers and the blanks.
4. The columns match evenly — they should be uneven.
5. Some items give away answers to other items.

Chapter 6
PREPARING MASTERY TESTS

Objectives: When you complete this chapter, you will be able to:
1. Select a mastery standard for a given unit and defend that standard.
2. Decide whether unit or objective-by-objective mastery is most appropriate for a given unit.
3. Prepare two mastery tests which are parallel in content and form.

THE previous chapter reviewed some of the basic principles of educational testing and measurement which are applicable to mastery learning. Beyond these basics are several areas that must be considered to insure the effective use of evaluation in ECE. This chapter deals with several key testing decisions which must be made prior to instruction.

The last chapter emphasized the importance of matching objectives with the most appropriate measurement device. Although some of your Essential objectives and many of your Enrichment objectives will best be evaluated by using checklists or rating scales, in this section it will be assumed that the measurement device most appropriate for your Essential objectives will be a set of test items.

CRITERIA FOR MASTERY

Next to the problem of deciding what skills and/or content areas are essential, one of the most difficult decisions is choosing what evidence you will accept as proving that a student has indeed mastered the objectives. This decision will be resolved by the selection of an appropriate mastery level. In Chapter Three you learned to write performance levels for your objectives. But what is an appropriate level for mastery? There is no easy answer to this question, but some basic guidelines may help in selecting a level with which you will be comfortable.

1. As a rule of thumb, a mastery level should be somewhere between eighty-five and ninety-five per cent.
2. One hundred per cent is probably too high for all but most basic or simple memory tasks such as listing the names of the nine planets in order.
3. Ninety-five per cent may be best for those simple tasks which are not affected by judgement errors. This level gives students a little room for "careless" or mechanical mistakes while requiring a high level of performance. A ninety-five per cent level is particularly important where a high level of mastery is required due to the nature of the learning task itself as in a lifesaving class.
4. Eighty-five per cent is the equivalent of a "B" in many school grading systems and thus it represents a relatively high standard while leaving some room for reasonable student error. This level will be most useful for higher level tasks.

At this point, one area of potential confusion needs to be considered. Some teachers and parents confuse mastery levels with grade level cutoff scores. Remember that when you set a mastery level, you are establishing how well you expect students to perform on the basic or Essential content of the course. An eighty-five per cent, therefore, does not mean a grade of B, it means that the Essential content has been mastered to an eighty-five per cent level. To receive a higher grade, students must complete some of the Enrichment activities.

ASSEMBLING THE TEST

An additional problem, which must be faced when setting mastery standards, is deciding whether you plan to require a particular level of performance on each objective as you did when you practiced writing performance levels, or whether you are willing to settle for adequate peformance on the overall test, knowing that a student may do well on some objectives and poorly on others. We call this distinction objective-by-objective mastery versus unit mastery.

Objective-By-Objective Mastery

Objective-by-objective mastery is most useful where each student is expected to master each objective at a designated level. In this case, a high level of performance on one objective will not compensate for poor performance on another. Objective-by-objective mastery is most useful at the elementary level and in those secondary classes which have a limited number of objectives and which require a wide variety of test items. The example below shows a pair of objectives followed by an objective-by-objective test to measure their mastery. Using this format, notice how it would be easy to spot which objectives have been mastered and which have not and thus to determine who needs what correctives work.

Sample Objective-By-Objective Test

Objectives:

Objective 1: The student will describe the function of 5 out 6 of the following plant parts:

pollen	phloem	xylem
ovary	cambium	pistil
root hairs	anther	meristem

Objective 2: The student will draw a simple flower and label each of the following structures:

anther	stamen	petal
pistil	stem	

Matching Test Items.

Objective 1: (mastery = 5 out of 6)
Define the funtion of each of the following plant parts:

   1. Xylem —
   2. Phloem —
   3. Cambium —
   4. Pollen —
   5. Pistil —
   6. Ovary

Objective 2: (mastery = 5 out of 5)

   Draw a clear diagram of a simple flower and label each of the following structures:

   7. Petal —
   8. Stem —
   9. Antler —
   10. Pistil —
   11. Stamen —

Unit Mastery

In some classes or units, teachers need to measure a student's knowledge of many details and facts. These tests will typically consist of a large number of similar items such as several long matching or numerous short answer items. In such cases, there may be little concern with whether a student masters each specific objective as long as the overall performance on the test is adequate. A test in which only the overall number of correct items is important is said to measure unit mastery.

Tests measuring unit mastery are easier to construct and grade but this ease is balanced by the greater difficulty in determining specific areas for correction. To reduce this difficulty, teachers using unit mastery should group items by objectives and sequence the groups based on the order in which the content was presented in class. With this approach, areas of particular difficulty can be spotted regardless of the type and level of mastery desired.

MAKING PARALLEL TESTS

Mastery tests must be prepared in pairs — one to follow Best Shot instruction and one to follow Corrective assistance. A pair of tests should be parallel in that each measures the objectives but is written in a slightly different form. The examples below show how tests can be varied without too much extra effort.

Writing Parallel Tests Items

If you want students to	*You can vary your tests by*
1. Define scientific items.	Sampling at least some different terms on each test.
2. Measure the length of objects.	Letting students measure different objects on each test
3. Name the capitals of all fifty states.	Presenting the states in a different order.
4. Name the original seven astronauts.	Varying or rephrasing the item

TEST LENGTH

One additional consideration in assembling mastery tests is test length. These tests need to be relatively short, say from twenty to forty-five minutes. Sticking to this time limit forces teachers into only testing the essentials and thus eliminating wasted time grading unnecessary items. This time-saving feature is essential in ECE since students will need to be placed into groups before Corrective instruction can begin.

COMPREHENSIVE EXAMINATIONS

There is nothing in the ECE model which would discourage the use of cumulative examinations administered at the end of a marking period or semester. In fact, such a practice would help in reinforce the Essentials. These tests should, however, be limited to Essential objectives.

Several suggestions will be helpful to those who would like to pursue the concept of cumulative mastery tests.

1. A cumulative mastery test need not measure all aspects of each

objective, but it should measure an adequate sample. The sample should represent the content and different congnitive levels covered during instruction.

2. Some brief review and drill should be provided to help students prepare for their examination.

3. Unit mastery will probably be the best way to evaluate these tests since, in most cases, no corrective activities will follow.

A further discussion of long-term or cumulative mastery tests will be found in Chapter Ten. Most teachers who are new to ECE, however, will probably prefer to delay consideration of cumulative testing until they have developed and implemented several individual units. With more and more schools, districts and states going to some type of criterion-related testing, the use of cumulative mastery tests in each class should become increasingly important.

Chapter 7
BASIC INSTRUCTIONAL PRINCIPLES

Objective: When you complete this chapter, you will be able to incorporate each of the following nine instructional principles into your instruction:
1. Increased Academic Learning Time
2. Perceived Purpose
3. Shared Objectives
4. Practice and Feedback
5. High Success Rate
6. Learning Style Adjustment
7. Mini-Max
8. Small Steps
9. Closure

NO matter how artistically written and intellectually defensible your objectives and tests, teaching ultimately depends upon your ability to cause students to learn. Although ECE focuses more on the design of instruction than it does with supporting any particular pedagogical techniques, a brief review of several new and/or well established instructional principles should help to improve instructional effectiveness. Most of these techniques will be particularly helpful during the Best Shot approach to Essential objectives.

ACADEMIC LEARNING TIME

Current research on effective schools has brought to light one seemingly obvious yet often overlooked aspect of learning — how time is actually spent in classrooms.* This concern for the utilization of classroom time is usually considered under the heading of "academic learning time" or ALT for short.

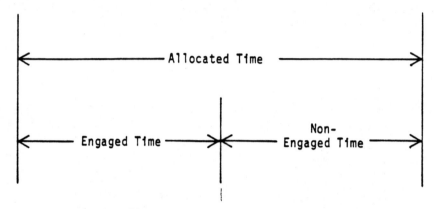

Figure 2. Academic Learning Time

Consideration of ALT begins with determining how much time is potentially available for learning. This available time is called "allocated time." As can be seen on Figure 2, some of the allocated time is going to be used in classroom management, socialization, discipline and other activities which are not primarily instructional. This part of the period during which students are not learning skills or content related to the particular course is called "nonengaged time." The actual time during which students are physically and/or mentally involved in tasks with which they are having a high degree of success is called "engaged time" or "time-on-task." Teachers who provide for higher engaged time can be expected to produce greater academic gains in their pupils.

Since most of the pioneering work on ALT was done at the ele-

*Squires, David A., Huitt, William G., and Segars, John K.: *Effective Schools and Classrooms: A Research-Based Perspective,* Alexandria, Ass'n for Supervision and Curriculum Development, 1983, pp. 113-119.

mentary level, the applicability of ALT research conclusions to secondary schools is currently suspect. It is nonetheless reasonable to assume that, regardless of level, teachers who keep students involved on tasks at which they are successful will have a greater chance of improving learning than those who spend class time in irrelevant activities. But knowing that increased engaged time can lead to increased learning does not prescribe teaching methods that will increase engaged time. The principles which follow should help in improving both engaged time and learning.

PERCEIVED PURPOSE

Students will stay on task longer when they perceive that what they are learning has meaning for them or will help them in some tangible way in the future. To be most effective, a statement of purpose or rationale should be both *personal* (relating directly and concretely to a situation in which the student could be or has been placed) and *immediate* (relating to events which are not too distant from the present moment). The statements below are examples of the attempts of three teachers to convince students that what they are going to cover is important for them.

1. "You need to study poetry for your own good."
2. "Studying poetry can imporve your communitive skills."
3. "Let's say you wish to tell a friend about something that happened to you in a special way. Could you make up a short poem to express your ideas? Let me show you an interesting example of what you will be able to do when we finish this poetry unit."

Notice that the first statement is neither personal (no concrete advantage is provided) or immediate (no indication of when or how poetry can be used). The second statement is mildly personal and immediate. The last statement is both personal (it describes a situation a student may have faced or could face) and immediate (the situation could come up in the immediate future).

Statements of perceived purpose provide both direction and motivation. Students should receive some indication of purpose for every major unit, objective and learning event even though this may be difficult to do in some cases. Sweeping statements such as, "You need this for your own good," or "You will need this next year," rarely motivate anyone to learn. The use of extrinisic rewards, such as gold stars or free time, as motivators should be employed only with great caution. Although these devices can be used effectively in some situations, they tend to limit a student's potential for doing tasks that will not result in an obvious reward.

SHARED OBJECTIVES

When you were taught to write or select objectives earlier in this book, the primary focus was on using these objectives in planning. These same objectives can also be used to improve student learning by sharing them with students. This sharing of objectives helps to orient students to what will follow and to indicate areas that need careful attention.

The easiest way to provide objectives to students is to begin each class with a discussion or mention of just those objectives which will be pursued that day. These objectives should be stated in a form that can be easily understood by the student. Avoid using the specialized or technical wording that is often used in planning. The presentation of sample problems or products (projects, reports, posters, etc.) can help to clarify objectives. Also, if you are teaching a long lesson which is based on only a few objectives, be sure to refer to the objectives frequently during the course of a lesson. This practice will help students keep their goals clearly in mind.

Two warnings about the sharing of objectives should help you avoid common pitfalls. First, remember that students will have to be oriented to the use and meaning of objectives. Unless you take the time to provide this orientation, and often reorientation, many students will fail to perceive the value of objectives and will pay little attention to them. Experience has shown that students at all levels become more proficient at using objectives the more they work with them.

A second but related problem presents itself when teachers simply hand students a long list of objectives early in the year or semester and expect students to keep up with them. This approach will only work with responsible and motivated students who have had a great deal of experience with objectives and should therefore be avoided in all other cases.

PRACTICE AND FEEDBACK

During all three segments of ECE — Essentials, Correctives and Enrichment — practice should be a significant pedagogical component. Students should receive frequent opportunities for active practice on the skills and/or content prescribed by the objectives. In most cases, several practice opportunities during each class will probably be appropriate. Long presentations or lectures should be broken by practice problems and/or questions.

As you select these practice opportunities, keep in mind the type of task that the student will be asked to perform on the mastery tests. A common fault is giving students practice in one format, say multiple choice or true-false items, and then testing them in another format such as short-answer or completion. If you plan to test a student's ability to recall information, be sure to let him or her practice recall tasks.

Under traditional teaching methods, you would be encouraged to continue practicing and providing extra assistance until almost all of your students had mastered the work. With ECE you will be working more rapidly in the Best Shot phase of instruction. Students having problems during this phase will be given extra assistance during the Corrective phase.

Another equally important aspect of practice is making sure that students receive information concerning the accuracy of their responses. To be most effective, such feedback should be prompt (within one hour), specific (indicating the correctness of the response) and non-punitive (no penalties for not knowing or for incorrect responses). One simple, effective but underutilized technique for obtaining and providing feedback is to use a "thumbs-up" exercise. Here a teacher asks students questions that can be answered with two alternatives (yes-no, true-false or belongs-does not belong). Students show their knowledge to the teacher as they hold out their hands with either thumbs-up or thumbs-down. Students who do not know or who are unsure of an answer can so indicate by holding their hands out flat. A third response, thumbs sideways, can be used in situations where three choices are possible. Some examples of the use of the thumbs-up technique would be

- True-false questions in history.
- Whether a word in a sentence is an adverb or an adjective.
- Indicating which organisms are arthropods.
- Showing agreement or disagreement with steps in geometric proofs.
- Classifying things as animal, plant or mineral.

Typically, a thumbs-up drill is conducted by the teacher who asks questions, observes student responses as shown by their hands and reacts to class and individual patterns of responses. If students give correct responses, the teacher can just keep going. When an individual or a portion of the class has trouble, special attention can be given.

The thumbs-up approach may need to be modified to accommodate very young children. Since these students may be tempted to copy the group, having students hold up cards marked "yes" or "no" can reduce the possibility of copying.

HIGH SUCCESS RATE

One definite way to improve the amount of engaged time is to plan instruction so that students will be engaged in tasks on which they are having a high rate of success. This is especially true for academically weak students who will normally be less motivated and persistent. Really tough problems should be saved for stronger students and as an occasional "side trip" for weaker ones. Research continues to confirm the mastery learning principle that success leads to more success.

LEARNING STYLE ADJUSTMENT

Recently, more and more researchers and instructional specialists have been concerned with differences in how students learn. Although the approaches and conclusions of the investigators vary, all educators should be aware of learning styles and how they affect learners.

The number of different learning styles ranges from three to twenty-six depending on which investigator you read. Perhaps the most obvious learning style is in the area of modality. Some students learn best by seeing (visual) while others learn best by hearing (auditory) or doing (tactile/kinestetic). In the case of students who are struggling, it is especially important to try to provide alternative modalities for learning. Lecturing, for instance, primarily involves an auditory mode and will thus be less effective with tactile/kinestetic and visual students. In the next chapter, which deals with preparing Correctives, modalities will be incorporated into the planning. Allowance for learning style should also be taken into consideration during the Best Shot approach.

MINI-MAX

Mini-max is a short form of the principle which suggests that instructors eliminate distractors.

> *Mini*mize unessential information.
> *Maxi*mize essential information.

Although this principle appears obvious, it is surprising how much time is spent in some classes going over material or engaging in activities which are unrelated to course goals. Films and T.V. programs are often prime suspects for time-killing events in the classroom.

Certainly not all classroom diversions are detrimental to the learning process. Occasional jokes or interesting stories are appropriate as long as they do that detract from the lesson in a significant way. Time for affective concerns can be legitimately spent but it should be planned (when possible) and balanced with cognitive objectives.

SMALL STEPS

This principle is closely related to several of the ones previously discussed. "Small Steps" means that instruction should be broken up into small segments or "chunks" with some practice after each segment. The more difficult or complex the material, the more important it is to break it up.

CLOSURE

With the exception of inductive lessons, students should not be "left hanging" at the end of a class period. At the end of every lesson, something should be done to "pull it all altogether." This practice of consolidating learning at the end of a lesson is called closure. A short quiz, thumbs-up exercise, discussion or summary are common ways to provide closure.

A FINAL NOTE

Rather than present an exhaustive discussion of all of the instructional techniques which could be effective in ECE classes, only a few such techniques were introduced in this chapter and then only in a summary form. Many other techniques are compatible with the ECE approach. The major criteria for any technique, however, shoud be whether or not it produces learning.

Chapter 8
PROVIDING CORRECTIVES

Objective: When you complete this chapter, you will be able to suggest Correctives for Essential objectives which are similar in content yet different in manner of presentation.

I N spite of a teacher's best efforts, some students will not be able to demonstrate mastery after the initial presentation of the material. These students may have failed at mastery for one or more reasons: (1) they may lack background skills or information necessary to understand the material, (2) they need more time to learn or (3) they need a mode of presentation which is more in harmony with their preferred learning style. This chapter will present the principles related to determining and providing effective Corrective activities.

Before getting into the development of Corrective activities, a review of the overall flow of the Corrective track might be helpful. Figure 3 shows at a glance both the steps and decisions that must be made in the Corrective process. After a student is placed in the Corrective track, he will begin with those activities which have been designed to help remediate specific problems. Adequate time should have been allotted for this process. Corrective activities should include one or more practice sets with the teacher using the student's performance on these activities as a guide in deciding when the student is ready for the second mastery test. Deciding when the student

64

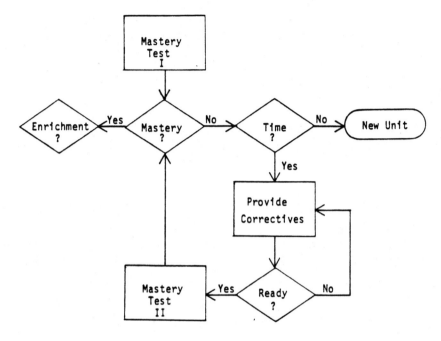

Figure 3. Overview of Corrective Cycle

is ready for this test is critical. You do not want to wait too long if you think the student is ready because this may deprive him or her of a chance for Enrichment opportunities. Offering the second test too soon, on the other hand, can lead to the student's inability to obtain mastery, thus leading to frustration and discourgement.

Based on their performance on Mastery Test II and time available, students might be allowed to proceed to the Enrichment track or to go back to additional Corrective activities. Students who are given a second chance by working in the Corrective track should be given a third mastery test at the completion of the unit. This test can be a third form of the mastery test or Mastery Test I. With proper monitoring of student practice exercises during the first Corrective cycle, however, few students should need a third chance at a mastery test. The number of times a mastery test is administered will be determined by the amount of time left in the unit and/or the teacher's willingness to give the test after the start of a new unit.

DECIDING WHAT TO CORRECT

In Chapters five and six, strong emphasis was placed on matching test items with objectives and grouping items by objectives. Such practices simplify the process of deciding who needs what Corrective assistance. Under normal circumstances, students will not be required to complete corrective activities for each individual item missed on the test. Rather, they will need such activities only for those objectives which were not mastered at the specific level. Deciding which objectives require remediation will be an easy task if the objective-by-objective approach has been used since the test format itself will show at a glance which objectives were not mastered. Teachers using the unit mastery approach may have a more difficult time deciding which objectives have not been mastered. These teachers will probably need to provide more Corrective activities than would otherwise be required to insure that students are in fact ready to take the second mastery test.

DEFICIENCIES IN BACKGROUND SKILLS

One problem which arises frequently in dealing with Correctives is that of the student with a lack of the background skills necessary to master a given unit. You might recall that one of the trade-offs with ECE was the elimination, in most cases, of any diagnostic testing. This sacrifice was made in an effort to increase the usability of the ECE approach in traditional classes. But what happens if significant deficiencies in background emerge after the first mastery test? What if the student lacks prerequisite skills as a result of one or more years of accumulated deficit?

While no simple solutions to this problem exist, steps can be taken to deal with the deficiencies. The first step would be to identify all those students who had problems on skill objectives as opposed to content objectives on Mastery Test I. Then, by studying these test results or results from some other informal assessment, the teacher should determine whether students have appropriate prerequisite skills. Students with deficiencies in the area of prerequisites should be provided with Corrective assistance in these areas if possible. The focus should be on strengthening just these skills which will allow students to reach mastery on the second mastery test.

DECIDING HOW TO CORRECT

Assuming that students possess the prerequisites necessary to learn a given unit, the process of providing Correctives is straightforward. The Corrective activities are provided for each missed objective but they should be presented using modalities, methods or materials which are different from those used in the Best Shot instruction. A wide variety of approaches is possible.

Below are some examples of how classroom instruction can be varied by both group arrangment and learning modality.

Examples of Possible Corrective Activities

I. Individual Correctives
   A. Auditory - tape recorded presentation
   B. Visual - additional reading material at an appropriate level
   C. Tactile - manipulative experiences such as measuring objects or assembling a map puzzle
II. Group-Paced Correctives
   A. Large Group
      1. Auditory - special lecture or tape recording
      2. Visual - films, transparencies, board work
      3. Tactile - hands-on experiments
   B. Small Group or Pairs
      1. Auditory - group discussion, quiz game, drill
      2. Visual - film strip viewing, peer demonstration
      3. Tactile - experiments or computer work

Peer tutoring is a powerful form of Corrective activity. The effectiveness of peer tutoring has been well established as helping both the student receiving the help and the tutor. Some preparation, however, can help to insure its effectiveness. One initial step would be to make sure that those who are tutoring are able to work well with others in general or at least during tutoring sessions. A second step would be to provide a brief training session for tutors in which they learn how to follow the three-step formula that follows.

1. **Diagnose the student's problem** — All too often, tutors explain something without determing the exact nature of the student's difficulty. Having the student explain what he knows or demonstrate what he can do will help tutors to spot areas of trouble.
2. **Demonstrate a solution or explain the area of difficulty** — The tutor must be patient and non-threatening. The use of alternative methods and/or modalities is often helpful.
3. **Have the student demonstrate mastery** — This step is frequently omitted. Just asking, "Do you understand?" or "Any questions?" often leads to trouble as students only think they have understood.

PLANNING CORRECTIVE ACTIVITIES

Correctives must be carefully thought out and planned before the unit begins. To be safe, at least two or three different activities should be developed for each objective. They should be carefully described in the mastery plan.

Each Corrective activity should be designed to help students master the objectives they failed to master. For this reason, it is normal to find students working on Correctives placed in subgroups based on objectives they missed. Grouping all of the Corrective students together should be limited to situations in which all students need to master the same objectives, orientation sessions and periodic sessions which are devoted to management concerns such as checking progress or planning additional testing.

The examples below demonstrate the relationship between objectives, test items, Best Shot instruction and Correctives. To improve simplicity, only a single representative objective is presented. Particular attention should be given to the similarities and differences between the Correctives and the Best Shot instruction.

Sample Corrective Activities: Secondary

Topic: The Southern Colonies (U.S. History)
Objectives: The student will list from memory the three major

economic activities of the Southern Colonies and explain briefly why each is important.

Sample test item: In the space provided, list the three major economic activities in the Southern Colonies and briefly explain why each is important.

Best Shot instruction: The students will read the information in their textbooks about the major economic activities of the Southern Colonies. After reading the information, the students will name the three major economic activities and briefly explain why each is important. Finally, the students will list on a practice quiz the three major economic activities of the Southern Colonies and tell why each is important.

Corrective 1: The teacher will give the students a card with one of the major economic activities listed. The students will then discuss the importance of this activity. At the end of the lesson, the students will list from memory the three major economic activities and tell why each is important. The students will then discuss their responses.

Corrective 2: The students will view a filmstrip on the major economic activities. A discussion will follow immediately after the filmstrip. At the end of the discussion, the students will list from memory the three major economic activities and give a brief statement about the importance of each one. The teacher will check the students' responses and return them within an hour.

Sample Corrective Activities: Elementary

Topic: The Four Basic Food Groups (Health - Second Grade)

Objective: Given a list of fifteen nutritional food items and a chart listing the four food groups, the student will correctly place at least twelve items under the food group to which they belong.

Sample Test item: Using this list of foods, write them on the chart under the food group to which they belong. (Sample portion of list: toast, apples, eggs, tomatoes, steak, etc.)

Best Shot Instruction: Review the chart for each food group and discuss the similarities and differences of the foods belonging to each group. To practice we will use 4 poster boards with just the names of each food group written on them and a shoe box filled with pictures of different types of foods. The student will pull out an item, name it, name the food group to which it belongs and then tape it on the correct poster. Variation: have written names of foods in shoe box.

Corrective 1: Concentration game: cards will consist of both the names of the food groups and names of different food items — students will match corresponding cards.

Corrective 2: Spin-wheel game: the wheel consists of sections labeled by the names of the food groups and/or food items — students spin the wheel and name either the corresponding food group or a corresponding food (whichever applies).

ADDITIONAL SUGGESTIONS

Initially, teachers will find working with students in the Corrective group more difficult and time consuming. Careful planning and implementation of Correctives can, however, be expected to pay big dividends. Several additional suggestions should improve the chances for success.

1. Be sure to provide students with an orientation to the Corrective process. Even if you went over the total ECE strategy in the beginning as you were supposed to, go back over the Corrective procedures with your Corrective group during your first few units. At least initially, these students will probably need more direction than the Enrichment group.
2. Before beginning any Corrective procedure, check to make sure that the students understand the objective they are pursuing and the procedures they are to follow.
3. Provide activities which permit an especially high success rate with your Corrective students. When possible, make these activities fun.
4. Use frequent checks or formative evaluations with your Corrective group. These checks may be informal (the teachers asks a question to an individual student) or formal (a short practice quiz is given). Don't assume that just because students are able to fill in worksheets that they have mastered the content in them.

5. Where skills and/or content above the knowledge (memory) level are involved, avoid training students to answer specific test items. Help students learn to apply or transfer skills to new situations.
6. Immediately prior to administering Mastery Test II, review all Essential objectives. This review will help students avoid missing items on the second test that they answered correctly on the first.

The assurance that all students who need it will be given additional help in mastering the Essential objectives is one of the attractive aspects of ECE. It is through the effective use of Corrective activities that almost all students will be able to earn a satisfactory grade through mastery of significant skills and information.

Chapter 9

PROVIDING ENRICHMENT

Objective: When you complete this chapter, you will be able to:
1. Prepare a set of Enrichment objectives.
2. Develop a set of grade cutoff scores related to performance on Enrichment objectives.
3. Select appropriate strategies for implementing Enrichment objectives.

THE special needs of students who master content and skills faster than their peers are frequently ignored or reserved for a highly select group of students who are labeled as being gifted and talented. Often, this group resorts to unproductive or disruptive behavior in an effort toward off boredom. By providing faster learners with opportunities for Enrichment, teachers can keep these students out of trouble while increasing the amount of educational opportunity and challenge they deserve. One particularly attractive feature of ECE is that all students have access to the Enrichment track. No student is permanently assigned to a "slow" group. In fact, it is expected that as students gain in their ability to master the Essentials over the course of a year, more and more will earn their way into the Enrichment group.

Students in ECE are allowed to begin Enrichment only after successful completion of one of the mastery tests. Those who reach mastery on the first test should have adequate time to complete all

Enrichment work. Students who must receive Corrective assistance and complete the second mastery test will have less time in which to complete Enrichment objectives.

Regardless of the time available, a list of objectives, often in sequential order, must be presented to the students in the Enrichment track. They then become responsible for working through each objective until it has been accomplished to the teacher's satisfaction. In most cases, only one objective will be pursued at a time. Upon successful completion of an objective, the student can check the time available and, if sufficient time remains, proceed to another objective. If no more time is available, the teacher has the option of allowing students to complete one or more objectives outside of class or receiving credit for the work already completed.

SELECTION OF ENRICHMENT ACTIVITIES

Most teachers have a good feel for what kinds of experiences could be enriching. Often these experiences are those topics or experiences that they would like to teach but never can get around to. We recommend that teachers begin their planning for Enrichment with a brainstorming session, just getting some ideas down. These activities or objectives will usually be classifiable as being one of three types: reinforcement, extension or exploratory.

Reinforcement Objectives/Activities

Some activites are primarily designed as *reinforcement*. These activities provide the student opportunities to strengthen Essential skills or to transfer them in a limited manner. Although reinforcement activities are not the most exciting Enrichment, they are frequently appropriate where Essential skills are being emphasized. The list below provides some examples of reinforcement activities:

1. Mastery students in mathematics can complete one or more of the more difficult exercise sets which are typically found at the end of practice sections in many texts.
2. In English composition, mastery students can write additional short reports (assuming one written report was required by the

Essential objectives) which may be longer or more complex than the earlier one.

3. Mastery students may be required to spell and define words for which they only had to match definitions and terms during Essentials instruction.

4. After completing Essential material on conducting experiments in science, mastery students can conduct additional experiments.

Extension Objectives/Activities

Teachers often find themselves wanting to go beyond the Essential material by providing opportunities for extensive transfer and additional depth. These types of Enrichment activities are *extension* activities. Several samples of extension activities are listed below:

1. In a unit on the American Civil War, mastery students may
   a. Prepare battle diagrams and use them to explain the course of one battle.
   b. Tape record a simulated live broadcast from the Appomattox Courthouse as it might have been done by one of the major networks.
   c. Interview one or more local history buffs to find out why the Civil War holds such interest for many Americans.
2. In a unit on community helpers in third grade social studies, mastery students may:
   a. Conduct tape recorded interviews with some community helpers to share with the class.
   b. Prepare a poster describing the role of one community helper.
   c. Read one book about a community helper (fiction or nonfiction) and write a brief report on it.
3. In a unit in American poetry in eleventh grade English, mastery students may:
   a. Read selected European poets and compare them to selected American poets to answer the question, "Is American poetry unique?"
   b. Read selected prose works by American poets and compare the quality of expression between the two forms.

Exploratory Objectives/Activities

A third type of Enrichment activity is *exploratory* in nature. These activities allow students to explore entirely new content, skills or experiencies which are not directly related to the unit at hand but which are relevant to the discipline under study. Some examples of exploratory acivities would be the following:

1. In a unit on The American Revolution, mastery students may study and report on the differences between primary and secondary sources of historical information along with what constitutes an historical fact.
2. In a unit on animal behavior in seventh grade science, mastery students may complete a self-instructional package on how to conduct an experiment.
3. Mastery students in elementary mathematics may be given an opportunity to pursue simple computer programs through flow charting.
4. Mastery students at almost any level could be allowed to work on special materials to develop problem solving and critical thinking skills.

PREPARING FOR ENRICHMENT ACTIVITIES

After listing a variety of possibilities for enrichment activities, you will need to consider an appropriate method for providing these activities. To be most effective, Enrichment should involve a range of group sizes and modalities. Some of the possibilities for providing Enrichment include independent student work and participation in small and large group instruction.

Sample Enrichment Activities by Group Size

Individual

Reports based on reading assignments or personal investigation
Student Activity Packages — Learning Activities Packages or Self-Instructional Packages can be read or heard via tape recording.
Learning Center Activities

Special worksheets
Work in textbooks, extra chapters in the assigned or an alternative text
Computer assisted instruction
Producing a radio (tape recorded) or TV show (video tape recorded)

Small Group

Group reports or projects
Viewing and reporting on a media presentation
Student-directed or teacher-directed seminars
Tutoring arrangments with non-mastery students on a limited basis

Large Group

Special lectures
Guest speakers
Special demonstrations

Several factors will limit the kinds of Enrichment activities that a teacher can prepare. The teacher's available time is one such factor. Time for planning and conducting lessons is always limited. Being mindful of this limit, teachers need to prepare just enough activities to meet the requirements for an A grade. Furthermore, at least during early attempts with ECE, the activities selected should be ones that require a minimum of teacher direction unless it is within a large group context.

The teacher's experience with using small group and individualized approaches to instruction is another limiting factor. Some prefer large group instructional settings, whereas others prefer individualized ones. Those who are inexperienced with individualized and small group teaching will probably need to move into these styles slowly.

Students differ in their abilities to perform in different instructional settings. The level of student responsibility constitutes a third limiting factor. For some, working alone is best, while for others, working in large structured groups is the only way they can learn. Teachers with a substantial number of students who cannot work well alone or in small groups must depend on large group Enrichment activities such as permitting everyone to watch and critique a film or listen to a brief high quality lecture.

Once a list of activities has been generated, the particular ones to be used should be selected based on your constraints and preferences. These activities must, of course, be stated as objectives. Be careful that each Enrichment activity has some defensible educational value. Offering activities just for the sake of offering activities can lead to some real public relations headaches.

As you select your activites, keep in mind that some students who go through the Corrective track will only have one or two class periods in which to complete additional grade-elevating activities; therefore, one or more of your objectives should be limited enough to permit completion within a period or two.

DEFINING STANDARDS FOR ACCEPTABLE PERFORMANCE

After the activities for Enrichment have been selected, they should then be written in behavioral terms. You will want to be extra careful to insure that the criteria for evaluating these objectives is clear. This step is of particular importance for individualized work. If considerations such as spelling, grammar or neatness are to be considered, the objective should say so. An evaluation might require students to take a test on some Enrichment reading assignments, but tests should be used only where the objectives call for them. Reports, seminars, posters, interviews and the like should be evaluated using a checklist or a rating scale. The example below was taken from a seventh grade social studies unit on prehistoric times. Notice the clarity with which the evaluation criteria are expressed.

Sample Enrichment Plan

Enrichment Objective: When given a list of famous archaeologists, the student will choose one and write a 3 to 4 page report describing his or her contribution to the study of man's past. The report will be neatly written in ink, in the proper format and with no spelling or major mechanical errors. To receive credit, the student will earn no less than 10 points on the rating scale.

Evaluation Procedure: Papers will be evaluated using the rating scale as follows.

Area	Poor	OK	Very Good
Content	1	2	3
References	1	2	3
Format	1	2	3
Neatness	1	2	3
Mechanics	1	2	3

Instructional Procedure: Students will be given a brief overview describing the appropriate procedures and format for writing a report. Sample papers from the previous year will be shown and then made available for use as references. Reports must include the use of at least 2 references, only one of which can be an encyclopedia.

The use of samples of previous students' work can be of significant value by clarifying tasks for students. To avoid outright copying, just eliminate the topic of the samples from the list of potential topics.

Be sure to be encouraging of all efforts on Enrichment activities. This does not mean that unacceptable work should be accepted, but constructive criticism, encouragement and an opportunity to improve on weaknesses should be provided.

SELECT A GRADING POLICY

A typical grading policy will require that students successfully complete so many Enrichment objectives for a grade of B and so many additional objectives to receive an A. The real problem is deciding how many Enrichment objectives are appropriate for each grade. The number will vary from class to class, depending on the total time available to students, the age and maturity of the students, and the teacher's experience with a particular grade and/or subject. Often, teachers will have a larger number of activities available than is required, thus permitting students a choice of which to pursue. Others may wish to make some particular Enrichment activities required for an A or B. Regardless of the number chosen, remember to have one or two that can be completed in a relatively short time. In the next chapter, you will be shown some of the more technical aspects of providing grades for Enrichment. The example which follows should serve to demonstrate an overall grading policy. Notice that Objective Five is the one enrichment activity that all students must complete to earn a B or A grade.

Sample Grading Policy

To Earn a grade of	*You must complete these tasks*
A	Complete all requirements for a grade of B. Complete three additional objectives Tutor for at least 1/2 hour.
B	Reach mastery on all Essential objectives. Complete any one Enrichment objective in addition to number 5.
C	Reach mastery on all Essential objectives.
D	Obtain a score of at least 70% on either mastery test.
F	Obtain a score of less than 70% on both mastery test.

In developing your grading policy, decisions have to be made about what to do with late, incomplete and inadequate assignments. Never accept work that is clearly substandard. Where time permits, allow students to correct and resubmit inadequate work, especially if it resulted from an honest misunderstanding. During initial trials of your Enrichment objectives, do not penalize students for misinterpretations based on unclear directions or objectives. A clear set of directions will help to eliminate this problem but remember that "clear to the teacher" is often quite different from "clear to the student."

Most teachers find the Enrichment part of ECE the most fun. They look forward to it because it gives them a chance to teach some of the "neat stuff" they may have wanted to get to for years and could not. It provides both students and teachers a chance to be creative. Attractive Enrichment options also have the effect of encouraging students to master the Essentials as soon as possible.

Chapter 10

GRADING AND RECORD KEEPING

Objective: When you complete this chapter, you will be able to develop a grading policy and a record keeping system to facilitate ECE.

GRADING students and maintaining records are often seen as necessary evils of teaching regardless of the type of instruction being used. The secret is to develop systems which complement, not detract, from worthwhile learning goals, while at the same time are simple to understand and maintain. Presented in this chapter are some issues and suggestions which will help to refine the grading policy which has been discussed previously.

DECIDING AN APPROPRIATE GRADE FOR MASTERY

What grade should students receive if they have mastered all of the Essential objectives to a high degree? Block and Anderson have recommended a system in which all students who master course objectives are given A's.* While their overall system is definitely sound, it does require a greater initial committment to mastery than

---

*Block, James H. and Anderson, Lorin W.: *Mastery Learning in Classroom Instruction*. New York, Macmillan, 1975.

many schools are willing or able to make. A more adoptable and functional approach would be to allow a C to represent mastery of Essential objectives. This approach can be justified in several ways. Teachers in many schools would consider it a major triumph if a majority of their students would master Essential material and truly earn C's. For many students, a grade of C, while not ideal, is a step in the right direction. There will also be a demonstrable but not insurmountable difference between the grades of A and C, thus reducing the possibility of grade inflation.

Further, if mastery is set at an A, it becomes possible in some situations for students to obtain a satisfactory grade of C or B without having mastered one or more objectives. We would suggest that once schools reach a point where a significant number of teachers are using mastery for all of their units under ECE, that teachers and administrators explore the possibility of using Block and Anderson's A mastery system. Any transition at that point would be relatively simple. One compromise between the two possibilities (A mastery vs C mastery) is to set the mastery of Essentials at the B level. No major problems are posed with this system other than the possibility of students receiving a C without having mastered the Essential objectives.

WORKING WITH STUDENTS WHO DO NOT REACH MASTERY

One of the significant features of ECE is that each unit will have a definite termination date. This allows the teacher to begin a new unit with whole class instruction every few weeks. Whereas this scheduling arrangement avoids the necessity of a completely individualized system, it does mean that time will inevitably be called before some students have reached mastery. What, if anything, can be done about these students?

Some teachers may need to play it "by the book," beginning and ending units for the entire class on a definite schedule. They may not be comfortable having students work on several units at once or may lack the skills necessary to manage such an arrangement. These teachers will need to develop a scale or policy which will help them decide which grade to give students who still have not reached mastery at the end of the unit. If, for example, mastery is going to be set at a C, then some definite criteria, such as the number of objectives still unmastered, should be used to determine D and F grades. The previous chapter showed a sample grading structure which provided for these slower students.

Other teachers find that their schedules, subject matter and/or tolerance level will permit them to allow students to continue the Corrective process beyond the formal ending date for the unit. They will usually permit students added time to master the Essentials even though all of the students in the class will have begun the next unit. These "overlap" students must complete the Corrective work on their own during free periods, lunchtime or after school. Under ideal conditions, students would be able to continue to pursue a set of objectives until it is mastered. Few teachers, however, have time to provide this level of individualized assistance.

DETERMINING SUMMARY GRADES

Thus far, the emphasis has been on determining a student's achievement in each unit. At the end marking period, however, individual unit grades must be pulled together to yield some summary mark which will then go on a report card. This summary or combining process is a relatively simple one and actually requires less time than traditional "averaging" approaches.

In order to combines grades, letter grades will need to be converted to numbers. To determine a summary grade, the following steps should be followed:

1. Convert each unit grade to a numerical value (usually a percentage) which is equal to the highest number in that letter grade range. In the case of the F grade, the teacher will need to use his or her best judgement as to what value to use. A lower limit should be set on the F to give slow students some chance to improve their grades in subsequent units. The chart below provides a possible conversion scale.

Unit Grade	School Grade Range	Unit Percentage
A	100-94	100
B	93-85	93
C	84-77	84
D	76-70	55-69

2. If a traditional or non-mastery unit is used, combine the component grades of that unit to yield a single percentage grade. If, for example, a partical unit involved two tests and several pop quiz scores, a unit average would be computed as shown below.

Component	Percentage Grade
Test 1	83%
Test 2	77%
Pop Quiz Average	80%

Combined scores (average $= \dfrac{240}{3} = 80\%$
for non-mastery unit

3. Average the resultant percentages for each unit.

Unit	1	2	3
Approach	Mastery	Traditional ·	Traditional
Source of score	Mastery-Percentage	Combine separate grades	Combine separate grades
Grades	100%	83% + 77%	96% + 87% + 90%
Unit avg.	100%	80%	91%

Six Weeks grade — Unit 1 100%
Unit 2 80%
Unit 3 91%
Exam $\dfrac{96\%}{367}$

Summary Grade $= \dfrac{367}{4} = 91.8\% = 92\%$

One alternative method of combining unit grades is possible if all of the units in a marking period are mastery units. A summary grade can be determined in this case by using the letter grades and omitting any conversion to percentages. The chart below displays one possible policy for combining grades.

Policy for Combining Grades

To Earn a Grade of	You Must Have
A	A's on all units
B	All B's and A's or an A to balance any C
C	All C's or better, or a B or an A to balance any D or F respectively
D	Mastery of at least one unit
F	Failure to master any units

In developing a grading policy, remember that the number of times it takes a student to reach mastery should have no influence on his or her grade. Students should not be penalized for taking additional time or opportunities to complete work.

AN ADDITIONAL CONSIDERATION FOR ENRICHMENT

Thus far, Enrichment has been treated as an all-or-none proposition: either a student receives a B or an A. But what can be done about students who, at the end of the unit, have not completed all of the objectives required for a higher grade? There are two possible answers to this question which are not necessarily mutually exclusive.

One solution, which follows the pattern discussed in the previous section on Correctives, is to provide some form of time extension (outside of class) for those who need it to achieve the next highest grade. Thus, a student who might need one extra objective to earn a B would be permitted to complete that objective outside of class.

A second solution, which could be used along with or instead of the first, is to provide some credit for each objective completed. As an example, let us look at a possible plan which could be used in one classroom in a school which has the following grade level cut-offs:

$$A = 100\text{-}94$$
$$B = 93\text{-}85$$
$$C = 84\text{-}77$$
$$D = 76\text{-}70$$
$$F \quad \text{Below } 70$$

Let us further assume that students who reach mastery will be given a percentage grade of eighty-four when grades are combined at the end of the marking period. If, in a given unit, the teacher wished to use three objectives to qualify students for a B and two more for an A, then a scale such as the one below could be used to convert each objective into a percentage grade. Notice that with the exception of the fifth and final objective, each succeeding completed objective earns the student three percentage points.

Incremental Credit for Enrichment Objectives

Requirement	Increment	Percentage Score	Grade
Mastery of Essentials	—	84%	C
Mastery + 1 Objective	3	87%	B
Mastery + 2 Objectives	3	90%	B
Mastery + 3 Objectives	3	93%	B+
Mastery + 4 Objectives	3	96%	A
Mastery + 5 Objectives	4	100%	A+

In other situations, the size of the increment can be changed to correspond with the number and difficulty of the Enrichment objectives. By using this system, some credit can be given for each objective completed. Thus, if time prevents students from completing all three objectives to earn a maximum B, then at least they can earn a low or medium B with the completion of additional objectives. Notice that, although the letter grade for the unit may not reflect the exact number of objectives completed, this number will have an influence on the percentage score and thus the summary grade.

RECORD KEEPING

A well planned system for keeping track of student progress can go a long way toward reducing a teacher's workload. Teachers using ECE should keep a record sheet for *each unit.* The sheet should be structured more or less like the traditional grade book page with the elements to be recorded written as column headings. In addition to grade book entries, some teachers like to keep a large classroom chart which allows students to keep track of their own progress. Regardless of where the results are recorded, eight elements need to be accounted for. These elements usually require separate columns on a record sheet or chart. They are presented below in the order in which they should be recorded.

1. **Essential Objectives** — At least one column should be provided for each Essential objective. These columns will be used to record the results of the practice exercises and homework assignments for each objective which in turn will provide some information for preliminary diagnosis of future problems as well as providing information which is useful in determining Corrective experiences.

2. **Performance on Mastery Test I** — Scores in this column will indicate the effectiveness of the initial instruction of the Essential objectives. More importantly, they will determine the grouping pattern for the next phase (Correctives or Enrichment) of ECE. These scores will be expressed in one or two ways. If objective-by-objective mastery is being used, then a student's score can be expressed as a fraction with the denominator representing the total number of objectives required and the numerator representing the number of objectives mastered by the student. If unit mastery is being used, then a percentage score will be sufficient.

3. **Correctives or Enrichment** — This column will contain a C or an E to indicate whether the student will begin work in the Corrective or Enrichment group respectively. This notation provides an instant summary which is often a time saver.

4. **Corrective Analysis** — One or more columns need to be devoted to indicating the specific objectives which will need to be mastered. These columns will remain blank for those students in the mastery group. The information in these columns is particularly useful since it provides the teacher with a record of which students belong in which Corrective group. It will even indicate if some objectives do not need any Corrective work at all. Some teachers find it more helpful to leave the room to write in the results of Corrective practice exercises as this information can assist in making grade decisions if students fail to achieve mastery on the second mastery test.

5. **Enrichment Objectives** — One or more columns should be used to record a student's completion of the various Enrichment objec-

tives. Normally, a check mark is adequate for indicating satisfactory completion. Unmarked columns indicate uncompleted objectives.

6. **Performance on Mastery Test II** — The scores in this column will indicate (1) who is ready for Enrichment and (2) who needs additional Correctives.

7. **Final Letter Grade** — This grade will provide an overall evaluation of the student's performance on the unit.

8. **Percentage Grade** — If the final letter grade is going to be converted into a percentage grade for the purpose of determining a summary grade, this is where it can be recorded.

Although the final form of the record keeping sheet may vary somewhat, the inclusion of the preceding eight elements should provide adequate information for both classroom management of groups and grading. It should be mentioned here that personal computer programs are currently available to handle most if not all of these elements conveniently and quickly.

EVALUATING LONG-TERM MASTERY

The instructional approach developed thus far should insure short-term mastery. That is, students should master content and skills at least long enough to successfully complete one of the mastery tests. It is consistent with the mastery approach in general and ECE in particular to require students to take a cumulative mastery examination over all Essential objectives in a marking period, semester or course. These objectives will probably only be sampled but any such sample should be representative of the number and importance of the objectives.

Long-term mastery examinations can be useful in documenting the success of the instructional approaches used. The pattern of results can suggest subsequent action. If students do poorly on the cumulative examination, opportunities for frequent review of completed objectives can be provided during each subsequent unit. If students do poorly only on certain objectives, different means can be used to teach, test and/or review these objectives with greater efficiency. If students do well, brag about it!

Class: World History

Semester: Fall 1983

Unit: The Renaissance

Students	Essential Objectives 1 2 3 4 5	Mastery Test I	C/E	Correctives Needed 1 2 3 4 5	Enrichment Completed 1 2 3 4	Mastery Test II	Letter Grade	Percent Grade

Figure 4. Sample Record Keeping Sheet

Chapter 11

IMPLEMENTING ECE

Objective: When you complete this chapter, you will be able to plan an orientation for an ECE unit.

THIS final chapter was prepared for those readers who are actually going to use ECE. The information provided should provide the finishing touches necessary to insure the best possible success.

ORIENTATION

Since ECE is very different from the instructional plans used in most classrooms, special effort must be made in the beginning to make sure students are comfortable with the system. The comfort will come from familiarity. Experience has shown that after about one unit, even primary grade students can follow the system and "talk the language".

The most obvious time for major orientation efforts is immediately prior to the first unit. At this time several areas need to be covered with students:

1. Students need to be told that a new type of teaching will be used which should allow them to learn more and consequently receive higher grades.

2. An overview of the system should be provided using a flow chart or diagram. Although all of the technical points and details need not be covered, each major step needs to be explained carefully.
3. The grading system must receive careful attention, especially with older sudents. A class grading chart would be extremely helpful at this time.
4. The increased responsibility of the student should be emphasized early.
5. When possible, samples of mastery materials should be displayed.
6. Above all else, teachers need to be positive about their expectations for the students and these expectations must be shared with the students.

The major orientation for the Corrective and Enrichment tracks should be provided after students have been grouped following the first mastery test. This will insure that students are not wasting time being oriented to procedures which are not germane. Students who begin Enrichment off-cycle or after having completed some Corrective work will need orienting to the Enrichment track but this can often be conducted by students already working in Enrichment.

AN IMPLEMENTATION CHECKLIST

With all of the initial work required to use ECE for the first time, it is helpful to have some means of keeping track of your progress as you procede. The checklist which follows should provide a means of keeping track of the most significant considerations.

Implementation Checklist

1. **Orientation:**
   _____ Have I made plans to orient the students to the overall process or flow of ECE?
   _____ Will my presentation be simple enough for the students to understand?
   _____ Have I planned to show students how they can achieve more and earn higher grades?

2. **Content:**

_____ Have I eliminated content that might be considered irrelevant?

_____ Have I included content which will be useful either as "building blocks" to other content or adaptive to "real life" situations?

3. **Objectives:**

_____ Are all my objectives clearly stated i.e., (a) are they in behavioral form and (b) do they contain condition and performance components?

_____ Are too many of my objectives written at the Memory Level?

_____ Have I included higher level objectives?

4. **Tests:**

_____ Do my test items match my objectives?

_____ Have I followed the rules in making out a good test?

_____ Is my mastery standard clear?

5. **Correctives:**

_____ Are students grouped according to either common scores on Mastery Test I, learning modality or objectives missed?

_____ Are my Corrective procedures different from my Best Shot method of teaching?

_____ Have I included a variety of teaching approaches?

6. **Enrichment:**

_____ Will the Enrichment activities challenge the students?

_____ Do I offer each student a variety of choices as to activities and/or objectives?

_____ Does my Enrichment truly enrich or is it a repetition of the Essential content?

_____ Are the conditions and criteria for successful completion clearly stated?

REDUCING THE WORKLOAD

Most teachers are at first overwhelmed by the amount of planning that is required in a mastery system such as ECE. Mastery does require a significant amount of planning in the beginning. The suggestions which follow can help reduce the amount of work necessary to successfully implement ECE:

1. Begin by developing a few mastery units. Do not start by trying to develop all of the units necessary for a year. Unless you are provided with extensive release time, plan to phase in your mastery units over a period of several years.
2. Field test your first unit before you prepare your second unit. You will learn a lot of valuable information from your initial successes and failures.
3. Initiate a "mastery unit cooperative" in your school or district. Adapt units from the cooperative to your classroom needs.
4. Try a team approach. Develop units in pairs thereby reducing the workload by half.
5. Utilize student helpers and peer tutors to free you to work with special problems.
6. Develop or select self-paced, programmed or self-instructional materials for use in the Corrective and/or Enrichment tracks.
7. Consider the use of classroom computers for Correctives, Enrichment and record keeping.

THE REVISION PROCESS

Any instructional materials, no matter how soundly conceived and conscientiously implemented, need to be evaluated and revised periodically. ECE units are no exception. Feedback to improve units is typically derived from an analysis of objectives not mastered, interview data and responses on student questionnaires.

The overall system of ECE can also be evaluated but since there are already volumes written on program and systems analysis, these topics will not be covered here. Rather, we will suggest a possible student feedback sheet which could be used to obtain student perceptions of ECE or even traditional units. It should be useful for students above third grade level. For primary students, some of the same items could be read to the students and students could respond by marking smiley or frowney faces.

The "Student Feedback Sheet" which follows will provide a sample of the types of questions that can be asked in evaluating student perceptions of an ECE unit. The results of these feedback sheets should help improve both cognitive and affective aspects of instruction.

Student Feedback Sheet

Unit _____

Directions: Please do *not* sign this sheet. Answer all questions as honestly and fairly as you can.

1. Check any of the statements below (you may check more than one) which describe how you feel about this unit.

   _____too difficult   _____O.K.   _____fun

   _____too easy   _____super   _____just right

   _____turned me on   _____interesting   _____turned me off

   _____a waste of   _____terrible   _____boring
        time

   _____just like the   _____I learned a   _____confusing
        other units   lot

2. Complete these sentences:

   a. The part of the lesson that I really liked was

   _____

   _____

   b. The part of the lesson that I liked least was

   _____

   _____

Directions: After each following statement, circle YES if you feel that the statement describes what you or your teacher did during this unit. Circle NO if you feel that the statement does not describe what you or your teacher did during this unit.

3. I worked or paid attention during almost all of the unit   YES   NO
4. My teacher did things to keep me working or paying attention during the unit.   YES   NO
5. My teacher told me why the things we learned during the unit were important.   YES   NO
6. My teacher gave us clear directions and explanations about what we were supposed to do.   YES   NO
7. My teacher explained things again when I didn't understand.   YES   NO
8. My teacher told me when my answers were right or wrong.   YES   NO
9. The quizzes and practice work helped me to get ready for the test.   YES   NO
10. My teacher let me know exactly what I needed to study for the test.   YES   NO
11. The tests for this unit were fair.   YES   NO
12. My teacher worked hard to make sure I learned what was in this unit.   YES   NO
13. My teacher used almost all of the class period for learning we didn't waste time.   YES   NO
14. My teacher did things that made me want to work hard.   YES   NO
15. I feel that this unit helped me to be a better learner.   YES   NO
16. I feel that this unit made me like school more.   YES   NO

A FINAL WORD

Mastery learning and ECE work. The main factor which will determine whether they can work for you is your dedication to making them work. Of course support from colleagues and administration is also significant but it is in the individual classroom where the "tire grips the road." It is important that you not expect miracles at first. It will take time for the students and you to get used to a new way of doing things. Furthermore, given the overall public school environment and politics in many regions, it is not likely that all students will succeed at first under this or any system. It is realistic to expect, however, that a greater number of your students will succeed and with that success you can expect greater professional satisfaction.

Appendix I

SAMPLE ELEMENTARY MASTERY UNIT

Title of Unit: Addition and Subtraction Without Trading

Subject: Math

Grade Level: 3

Time Required: 3 Weeks

Prepared by: Teresa L. Gandy

ESSENTIAL OBJECTIVES

Objective 1: Given 12 single-digit addition facts, the student will write the sums with at least 11 correct.

Sample Test Item
$$\begin{array}{r} 5 \\ +\,5 \\ \hline \end{array}$$

Best Shot Intruction: In teaching the single digit addition, I will put 2 or 3 examples on the board and we will work them together as a class. I will emphasize that the answer in addition is called the sum. For practice exercises, they will work problems like the sample test item.

Correctives:
1. The students will be given a worksheet involving problems in the addition of 2 numbers. They can use toothpicks, matches, etc. to help them add.
2. The students will work in pairs using flashcards of the addition facts. One student can show the flashcard while the other answers. Then the students can switch places. Student tutors from the Enrichmet track will also be available for assisting in this activity.

Objective 2: Given 12 simple subtraction facts such as 10 - 8, the student will write the differences with at least 11 correct.

Sample Test Item:
$$\begin{array}{r} 12 \\ -3 \\ \hline \end{array}$$

Best Shot Instruction: In teaching basic subtraction facts, I will present several problems on the board to work with the class. I could also give subtraction facts to the class orally. Practice items with the problems such as:

$$\begin{array}{ccc} 16 & 11 & 13 \\ -5 & -4 & -8 \\ \hline \end{array}$$

Correctives:
1. The student will make his own set of flashcards on subtraction facts. Then a tutor from the Enrichment track can flip the cards for the student as he answers.
2. The student will play a game with subtraction facts. If the

problem is 15 - 6, the student starts at 15 on the game board and moves back 6 spaces and he should land on 9.

Objective 3: Given 4 addition problems with three one-digit numbers, the student will find the sum with 100% accuracy.

Sample Test Item: $2 + 3 + 1 =$ _____.

Best Shot Instruction: When teaching the addition of three one-digit numbers. I will demonstrate a problem on the chalkboard. I will remind the students to find the sum of two numbers first and then add the third. Practice exercises will be examples such as: $5 + 8 + 4 =$ _____. We will do the first 2 or 3 together to make sure everyone understands before assigning other exercises.

Correctives:

1. The students will use toothpicks to help them find the answers to the problems given on the board.
2. The students will draw pictures representing the addition problems such as $2 + 3 + 1 =$ _____.

□ □ + □ □ □ + □ = _6_.

Objective 4: Given 10 two-digit number problems without trading, the student will write the sum or difference for each problem with at least 9 correct.

Sample Test Item:
$$\begin{array}{cc} 30 & 50 \\ +30 & -20 \\ \hline \end{array}$$

Best Shot Instruction: In teaching addition or subtraction without trading using two-digit numbers, I will present a problem on the board first. I will demonstrate the steps used when working each problem. Next, I will give the students a problem to work and check each student's answer to see if there are any problems. Practice exercises will be exactly like the sample test items.

Correctives:

1. The students will use toothpicks to help them add or subtract. The problems will be given on the chalkboard.
2. The students will work in pairs. One student can work a problem while the other checks his answer. They can switch places. Problems will be from an old textbook.

Objective 5: Given 2 word problems involving addition or subtraction, the student will solve both problems correctly.

Sample Test Item: You have 2 blue cars and 3 red cars. How many cars in all?

Best Shot Instruction: In teaching children how to solve word problems using addition and subtraction, I will remind the students of problem-solving tactics. I will put a problem on the board and we will work the problem using the tactics. For practice, I will have the students work one problem at a time and I will check their answers. After each child seems to understand the process of problem solving, I will let them do examples by themselves.

Correctives:

1. Students will work with the teacher doing the following pricing activity. Label two items with prices such as ruler + $9\frac{1}{3}$ and a pencil = $6\frac{1}{3}$. Give the child money equaling $15\frac{1}{3}$. Then ask the students questions such as: How much will it cost to buy a pencil and ruler? I will write the problem $9\frac{1}{3} + 6\frac{1}{3} = 15\frac{1}{3}$ on the board. Several problems like this could be used.

2. I will write pairs of information on the chalkboard such as:

3 brown dogs	6 oranges
9 white dogs	2 apples

   Then I will ask 2 questions about each pair, such as "How many dogs in all?"

ENRICHMENT OBJECTIVES

Objective 1: The student will construct a test on the Essential objectives and include the answer key. The student must rate at least 6 on the rating scale to have an acceptable grade on this objective.

Evaluation Procedure: A rating scale will be used on each student who completes the objective. They will be given points in each area.

1 - Unsatisfactory Work
2 - Satisfactory Work
3 - Excellent Work

Total points must be six or above with no less than two on any area.

	Mary	Jimmy	Keith	Hope	Ann
Neatness					
Variety of Problems					
Correctness of Answer Key					

Instructional Procedure: I will give the students a copy of the rating scale and explain to them exactly what is required of them in each area: Neatness = problems presented neatly, Variety of Problems = several different types of problems like the ones presented in the Essential objectives, and the answer key should be correct. The students will construct the test and answer key on two different papers. After I have checked the test and key using the rating scale, the students can switch tests to work. Then they can grade the tests, using the answer keys they made.

Objective 2: Given 25 addition and subtraction facts with a missing addend or subtrahend, the student will find the missing number with at least 23 correct.

Evaluation Procedure: The students will be tested at the end of the instructional period. They will be given 25 facts with missing numbers and the student will find the missing number. Twenty-three must be answered correctly.

Sample Test Item 9 - _____ = 6

Instructional Procedure: The students will be given a worksheet on this type of problem and they can work alone. The worksheet will include directions and a sample problem. If they have no problems with the worksheet, then they will be tested.

Objective 3: Given 25 addition and subtraction exercises that include parenthesis, the student will find the missing numbers in each problem with at least 23 correct.

> Evaluation Procedure: The students will be tested after the instruction. They will be given 25 problems on the chalkboard to copy and insert the missing number. At least 23 must be done correctly.

> Sample Test Item $(3+2) +$ _____ $= 7$.

> Instructional Procedure: I will introduce this objective with a worksheet. The directions and a sample problem will be shown on the worksheet. If they need further explanation, I will be available. When the worksheet is completed correctly, the student will be tested.

Objective 4: Given an addition or subtraction fact such as $12 - 3 = 9$, the student will write a word problem that the fact solves with 4 out 5 correct.

> Evaluation Procedure: The student will be given 5 facts and will be asked to write one word problem using each fact. The student will not be graded on spelling, punctuation, or grammar. The only criterion for the word problem is that the information in the word problem must correspond exactly to the fact presented. If the fact is addition, the problem must include addition of something. The same numbers must be used.

Instructional Procedure: To introduce this objective, I will give a fact on the board and the students will orally give a word problem about the fact. I will write the problem on the board as they dictate it. For practice, I will orally give them 5 facts to write problems for. If there are no problems, I will go over it again and give more practice.

Addition and Subtraction
Without Trading
(Mastery Test I)

Name _____   (Circle Track)
                                                  Mastery
Date _____   Non-Mastery

I. **Objective 1:** (mastery = out of 12)
   Directions: Add and write the sum.

1. 5	2. 3	3. 8	4. 7	5. 8	6. 2
+5	+6	+8	+9	+4	+9

7. 7	8. 7	9. 4	10. 9	11. 9	12. 8
+6	+8	+6	+5	+9	+9

II. **Objective 2:** (mastery = 11 out of 12)
   Directions: Subtract and write the answer.

13. 10	14. 12	15. 17	16. 15	17. 15	18. 13
-8	-3	-8	-7	-9	-8

19. 11	20. 10	21. 13	22. 12	23. 16	24. 11
-3	-4	-6	-5	-7	-7

III. **Objective 3:** (mastery = 4 out of 4)
   Directions: Add and write the sum.

25. 6 + 3 + 4 = _____.   27. 4 + 1 + 9 = _____.
26. 5 + 3 + 3 = _____.   28. 2 + 8 + 7 = _____.

IV. **Objective 4:** (mastery = 9 out of 10)
   Directions: Add or subtract and write answer.

29.	40 +40	30.	20 +70	31.	80 -70	32.	90 -60	33.	70 -40

34.	25 +52	35.	61 +37	36.	75 -54	37.	99 -29	38.	83 -42

V. **Objective 5:** (mastery = 2 out of 2)
   Directions: Add or subtract to solve the problem and write the answer.
   Problem: You have 2 blue cars and 3 red cars.
   39. How many more red cars than blue cars? _____.
   40. How many cars in all? _____.

Addition and Subtraction
Without Trading
(Mastery Test II)

Name _____   (Circle Track)
                                   Mastery
Date _____   Non-Mastery

I. **Objective 1:** (mastery = 11 out of 12)
   Directions: Add and write the sum.

| 1. | 9
+9 | 2. | 3
+7 | 3. | 5
+6 | 4. | 7
+9 | 5. | 9
+5 | 6. | 8
+7 |

| 7. | 7
+6 | 8. | 4
+6 | 9. | 2
+9 | 10. | 9
+8 | 11. | 6
+8 | 12. | 8
+4 |

II. **Objective 2:** (mastery = 11 out of 12)
   Directions: Subtract and write the answer.

| 13. | 12
-5 | 14. | 10
-2 | 15. | 15
-8 | 16. | 15
-9 | 17. | 15
-6 | 18. | 11
-4 |

| 19. | 13
-8 | 20. | 14
-8 | 21. | 12
-3 | 22. | 16
-7 | 23. | 12
-9 | 24. | 17
-8 |

III. **Objective 3:** (mastery = 4 out of 4)
   Directions: Add and write the sum.

25. $4 + 4 + 3 =$ _____.   27. $6 + 3 + 4 =$ _____.
26. $7 + 2 + 9 =$ _____.   28. $5 + 5 + 7 =$ _____.

IV. **Objective 4:** (mastery = 9 out of 10)
Directions: Add or subtract and write answer.

29. 40	30. 25	31. 90	32. 61	33. 70
+30	+52	-20	-37	-60

34. 62	35. 84	36. 67	37. 89	38. 56
+25	+15	-25	-17	-23

V. **Objective 5:** (mastery = 2 out of 2)
Directions: Add or subtract to solve the problem and write the answer.

Problem: There are 7 red stripes and 6 white stripes on the United States Flag.

39. How many stripes in all? _____.

40. How many more red stripes than white? _____.

GRADING POLICIES AND PRACTICES

Grading Policy

To earn a (n)   you must

    A   reach mastery on all Essential objectives and complete 4 Enrichment objectives.

    B   reach mastery on all Essential objectives and complete 3 Enrichment objectives.

    C   reach mastery on all Essential objectives.

    D   reach mastery on at least 3 out of 5 Essential objectives.

    F   master only 2 or less of the Essential objectives.

Plans for Students Who Fail to Meet Mastery

Students who do ot meet mastery on Mastery Test II can do more on their own if they want to elevate their grade. If there is time, I will work with these students. However, I will go ahead and begin the next unit.

Appendix II

SECONDARY MASTERY UNIT

Title of Unit: The Renaissance

Subject: World History

Grade Level: 10

Time Required: 3 Weeks

Prepared by: Bob Heaberlin

ESSENTIAL OBJECTIVES

Objective 1: The student will list five Renaissance writers and give one example of each of their works.

> Sample Test Item: In the blanks below list five Renaissance writers and one of their works. (Mastery ¾ 5 out of 5)
> *Writer*   *Work*
> 1. _____   _____

> Best Shot Instruction: In teaching the Renaissance writers, I will hand out a worksheet with a list of the various writers. The students will use their textbook to research the writers. Included in the research will be lists of books, contributions, and a summary about each writer. We will then hold a group discussion to talk about each writer.

> Correctives:
> 1. A student who passed Mastery Test I may work as a tutor on a one-to-one basis with students needing help on this objective. Together they can look up the writers in the book and work out a drill to call out writers and their works until the student feels that he knows them.
> 2. The student can work a crossword puzzle prepared by me on Renaissance writers.

Objective 2: When shown a set of 10 Renaissance paintings, the student will correctly name at least 8 of the paintings and state the name of the artist for each one.

> Sample Test Item: In the blanks below, write the name of the painting that I hold up and the name of respective painter of the painting. The paintings will be numbered 1-10 and you will be given 10 seconds to look at each painting. (8/10 mastery)
> *Painting*   *Artist*
> 1. _____   _____

> Best Short Instruction: In teaching Renaissance painting and painters, I will show Renaissance art by using Gould's *Early Renaissance: Fifteenth Century Italian Painting* and Borea's *The High Renaissance* books. In presenting each painting, I will discuss its unique qualities and provide the students

with a short biographical description of each artist. During the discussion, the students will take notes. At the end of the lecture I will hold up each painting and ask students at random to give me the name of the painting and its artist.

Correctives:

1. A student who passed Mastery Test I will serve as a tutor for the student who is doing remedial work. The tutor will drill the remedial student by going over the paintings and having the remedial student identify each painting and its artist.

2. Students will be placed in a group and each student will be assigned one Renaissance painting to research. The group will meet together and each student will display his/her assigned painting, discussing its qualities and identifying the artist.

Objective 3: The student will name at least one contribution of each of 5 scientists of the Renaissance period.

Sample Test Item: List a contribution for each of the following Renaissance scientists:

1. Harvey - _____

Best Shot Instruction: In studying Renaissance scientists, I will write the name of the scientists on the chalkboard and have the students use their testbooks to find their individual contributions to science. As a class, we will discuss each scientist and his contributions to science. As a class, we will discuss each scientist and his contributions.

Correctives:

1. The student will work a crossword puzzle prepared by the teacher on Renaissance scientists.

2. The student will review his/her notes on Renaissance scientists. I will then give him/her a hand-out sheet with a matching exercise to practice identifying scientists and their contributions.

Objective 4: Given a list of 3 Renaissance cities, the student will describe the importance of 2 of them as related to the Renaissance movement.

Sample Test Item: Describe the importance of the following

Renaissance cities as related to the Renaissance movement:

1. Milan - _____

Best Shot Instruction: In teaching the cities of the Renaissance, I will use a wall map of Italy to point out the location of each city. I will then write the names of the cities on the board and have each student research the contributions and importance of each city in their textbooks, encyclopedias, or library books. Following the reserch, we will discuss, as a class the students' findings.

Correctives:
1. I will give out a fill-in-the-blank worksheet to the students. Each question will give a description of a city and the student will have to name the city.
2. I will give each student a hand-out on the Renaissance cities with a summary of the importance of each. After providing the students with time to review the sheet, I will randomly ask the students questions about each city.

Objective 5: The students will define 8 of the following 10 vocabulary words dealing with the Renaissance. The words are: parchment, renaissance, orbits, anatomy, classics, elliptical, heliocentric, woodcut, movable type, and perspective.

Sample Test Item: In the blanks below, write a brief definition for each of the following words:

1. Parchment - _____

Best Shot Instruction: In teaching Renaissance terminology, I shall list the key words and a short definition on the chalkboard as we proceed through the lecture concerning contributions during the Renaissance. The students will list the terms and definitions in their notebooks as they are put on the board.

Correctives:
1. I will give the student a list of the words and he/she will look them up in the textbook and write the definition for each.
2. Students who need corrective work on this objective will be placed in one group. I will then give each student a list of the terms and their definitions. After the students are

given time to study the terms, they will compete against each other in a "bee" as I call out the term and the student gives me the definition.

ENRICHMENT OBJECTIVES

Objective 1: The student will write a two-page report on Gutenberg's printing press.

Evaluation Procedure: A rating scale of 1, 2, 3, 4 will be used to determine whether the student has met the criteria. Included in the paper should be a discussion on how the printing press popularized the ideas of the Renaissance, its effects on European civilization, and aspects of its further development. The paper must be written neatly in ink, in correct structure, and words must be spelled correctly. The student must attain a minimum score of 18 on the scale to meet the objective's requirements.

Item	*Poor*	*Fair*	*Good*	*Excellent*
Neatness	1	2	3	4
Grammar	1	2	3	4
Spelling	1	2	3	4
Ren. Ideas	1	2	3	4
Effects Civ.	1	2	3	4
Development	1	2	3	4

Instructional Procedure: The student will be told of the criteria requirements for the paper that he/she will be evaluated on. I will allow the student time to go to the library or time to work in class on the paper. Some of the library books that will be helpful to the student are *The Book: The Story of Printing and Bookmaking, Great Inventions,* and *The Reformation: "The Birth of Printing."*

Objective 2: The student will draw a map of Italy on poster paper and mark the five most important Italian Renaissance cities on the map.

Evaluation Procedure: A rating scale of 1, 2, 3, 4, will be used to rate the poster. A total of 12 points must be accumulated for the task to be acceptable.

Item	Poor	Fair	Good	Excellent
Neatness	1	2	3	4
Color	1	2	3	4
Cities	1	2	3	4
F o l l o w				
Directions	1	2	3	4

Instructional Procedure: The student will be told to use standard size poster paper and magic markers to complete the task. The student should use a variety of colors to make the map interesting. To find the 5 most important Renaissance cities the student should use his notes and textbook. The map of Italy in the textbook will serve as the model for the drawing. The cities should be indicated by marking a star and labeling each of the five cities.

Objective 3: The student will explain in his own words the intellectual movement in the Renaissance known as Humanism in a two-page essay.

Evaluation Procedure: The paper will be checked for correct spelling, neatness, and correct grammar. The student will be told to include any important dates, men, or contributions pertinent to Humanism in the essay. A scale of 1, 2, 3, 4, will be used to rate the paper. An acceptable score of 12 will be necessary to successfully complete the objective.

Item	Poor	Fair	Good	Excellent
Neatness	1	2	3	4
Spelling	1	2	3	4
Grammar	1	2	3	4
Imp. facts	1	2	3	4

Instructional Procedure: The student will be told of the criteria that will be evaluated. The student may use his/her notes, the textbook and any library book that might be helpful to research the topic. The student will be allowed time to go the library.

Objective 4: The student will construct a time line of the Renaissance period on the poster paper.

Evaluation Procedure: The student will use standard size poster paper and magic markers to complete the task. Included on the time line should be important dates concerning the men, ideas, accomplishments, and events of the Renaissance era. The poster should be done neatly and correct spelling is important. A scale of 1, 2, 3, 4 will be used to rate the student's performance. A total of 12 points is necessary for successful completion of the objective.

Item	Poor	Fair	Good	Excellent
Neatness	1	2	3	4
Follow Directions	1	2	3	4
Spelling	1	2	3	4
Dates	1	2	3	4

Instructional Procedure: The student will be told that he/she may use the textbook class notes or library books to research the dates for the time line. The student will be allowed time to go to the library to work on the objective.

The Renaissance
(Mastery Test I)

Name _____   (Circle Track)
                                                  Mastery
Date _____   Non-Mastery

I. **Renaissance Writers** (mastery = 5 out of 5)
In the blanks below, list five Renaissance writers and an example of each of their works.

Writer   *Example of Works*

1. _____   _____
2. _____   _____
3. _____   _____
4. _____   _____
5. _____   _____

II. **Renaissance Painting** (mastery = 8 out of 10)
In the blanks below numbered 1-10, write the name of the painting that I hold up and list its artist on the line next to it. The paintings will be numbered 1-10 and you will be given 10 seconds to look at each painting.

Painting   *Artist*

1. _____   _____
2. _____   _____
3. _____   _____
4. _____   _____
5. _____   _____
6. _____   _____
7. _____   _____
8. _____   _____
9. _____   _____
10. _____   _____

III. **Renaissance Scientists** (mastery = 5 out of 5)
Name one contribution made by the Renaissance scientists listed below.

Scientist   *Contribution*
1. Galileo   _____

2. Harvey   _____
3. Kepler   _____
4. Copernicus   _____
5. da Vinci   _____

IV. **Renaissance Citites** (mastery = 2 out of 3)

Describe the importance of the following cities as related to the Renaissance movement:

City   *Importance*

1. Florence   _____

                     _____

2. Milan   _____

                     _____

3. Rome   _____

                     _____

V. **Renaissance Definitions** (mastery = 8 out of 10)

Write a brief definition for each of the following words:

Term   *Definition*

1. parchment   _____

2. renaissance   _____

3. orbits   _____

4. anatomy   _____

5. classics   _____

6. elliptical   _____

7. heliocentric   _____

8. woodcut   _____

9. movable type   _____

10. perspective   _____

The Renaissance
(Mastery Test II)

Name _____   (Circle Track)
                                              Mastery
Date _____   Non-Mastery

I. **Renaissance Writers** (mastery = 5 out of 5)
In the blanks below, list five Renaissance writers and an example of each of their works.

Writer   *Example of Works*
1. _____   _____
2. _____   _____
3. _____   _____
4. _____   _____
5. _____   _____

II. **Renaissance Painting** (mastery = 8 out of 10)
In the blanks below numbered 1-10, write the name of the painting that I hold up and list its artist on the line next to it. The paintings will be numbered 1-10 and you will be given 10 seconds to look at each.

Painting   *Artist*
1. _____   _____
2. _____   _____
3. _____   _____
4. _____   _____
5. _____   _____
6. _____   _____
7. _____   _____
8. _____   _____
9. _____   _____
10. _____   _____

III. **Renaissance Scientists** (mastery = 5 out of 5)
Name one contribution made by the Renaissance scientists listed below.

Scientist   *Contribution*
1. da Vinci   _____
2. Copernicus   _____

3. Harvey _____

4. Kepler _____

5. Galileo _____

IV. **Renaissance Citites** (mastery = 2 out of 3)

Describe the importance of the following cities as related to the Renaissance movement:

City   *Importance*

  1. Florence   _____

            _____

  2. Genoa   _____

            _____

  3. Venice   _____

            _____

V. **Renaissance Definitions** (mastery = 8 out of 10)

Write a brief definition for each of the following words:

Term   *Definition*

  1. orbits   _____

  2. parchment   _____

  3. anatomy   _____

  4. elliptical   _____

  5. classics   _____

  6. renaissance   _____

  7. heliocentric   _____

  8. movable type   _____

  9. woodcut   _____

10. perspective   _____

GRADING POLICIES AND REQUIREMENTS

Grading Policy

To achieve a grade of "C" and proceed to the Enrichment objectives, a student must successfully meet the requirements of Mastery Test I.

The student who meets the criteria on the first test can proceed to the Enrichment objectives. If the student did not meet the criteria on the first test, then he must do Corrective work. The Corrective students are given Mastery Test II and, if they meet the criteria, they will receive a grade of "C."

To achieve a "B" grade a student must obtain mastery on one of the mastery tests and successfully complete the requirements for Enrichment Objectives 1 and 2.

An "A" grade may be achieved by the successful completion of the "B" requirements and the successful completion of Enrichment Objectives 3 and 4.

A student who has not met mastery on Mastery Test II will receive either a grade of "D" or "F". To achieve a "D" a student must meet mastery on 3 out of 5 Essential Objectives. An "F" will be given to those students who do not master at least 3 of the Essential Objectives.

Plans for Students Who Fail to Meet Mastery

A student who received a grade of "F" will be permitted to proceed to the next unit. If time permits, the student will be allowed to go back to the Renaissance unit and work on the objectives that he/she did not master. If the student successfully completes the work in a week, his/her grade will be raised to a "D."

BIBLIOGRAPHY

Block, James H. *Mastery Learning: Theory and Practice.* New York: Holt, Rinehart and Winston, 1971.

Block, James H. ed. *Schools, Society and Mastery Learning.* New York: Holt, Rinehart and Winston, 1974.

Block, James H. and Anderson, L. W. *Mastery Learning in Classroom Instruction.* New York: Macmillan and Co., 1975.

Bloom, Benjamin S. *Human Characteristics and School Learning.* New York: McGraw Hill, 1976.

Bloom, Benjamin S. *All Our Children Learning,* New York: McGraw Hill, 1981.

Bloom, B.S. Hasting, J.T. and Madus, G.F.: *Evaluation to Improve Learning.* New York: McGraw Hill, 1981.

Bloom, Benjamin. "Learning for Mastery." *Evaluation Comment 1.* 1968.

Carroll, John B. "A Model of School Leaning". *Teachers College Record.* 1963.

Educational Leadership. 37, 1979 (Issue devoted to Mastery Learning).

Frazier, Alexander. *Adventuring, Mastering, Associating: New Strategies for Teaching Children.* Washington, DC: ASCD, 1976.

Joyce, Bruce and Weil, Marsha. *Models of Teaching,* 2nd ed. Englewood Cliffs: Prentice-Hall, Inc. 1980.

Kounin, J.S. *Discipline and Group Management in Classrooms.* New York Rinehart and Winston, INc., 1970.

Lee, Jackson, F. Jr. and Pruitt, K. Wayne. *Writing Instructional Objectives: A Self-Instructional Approach.* Florence, SC: Francis Marion College Book Store, 1974.

Squires, David A., William Huitt and John Segars. *Effective Schools and Classrooms.* Alexandria: Association for Supervision and Curriculum Development, 1983.

Torshem, Kay Pomerance. *The Mastery Approach to Competency-Based Education.* New York: Academic Press, 1977.